ROUTLEDGE LIBRARY EDITIONS: EDUCATION 1800–1926

Volume 14

GEORG KERSCHENSTEINER

GEORG KERSCHENSTEINER
His thought and its relevance today

DIANE SIMONS

LONDON AND NEW YORK

First published in 1966 by Methuen & Co Ltd

This edition first published in 2017
by Routledge
2 Park Square, Milton Park, Abingdon, Oxon OX14 4RN

and by Routledge
711 Third Avenue, New York, NY 10017

Routledge is an imprint of the Taylor & Francis Group, an informa business

© 1966 Diane Simons

All rights reserved. No part of this book may be reprinted or reproduced or utilised in any form or by any electronic, mechanical, or other means, now known or hereafter invented, including photocopying and recording, or in any information storage or retrieval system, without permission in writing from the publishers.

Trademark notice: Product or corporate names may be trademarks or registered trademarks, and are used only for identification and explanation without intent to infringe.

British Library Cataloguing in Publication Data
A catalogue record for this book is available from the British Library

ISBN: 978-1-138-22412-4 (Set)
ISBN: 978-1-315-40302-1 (Set) (ebk)
ISBN: 978-1-138-21450-7 (Volume 14) (hbk)
ISBN: 978-1-138-21451-4 (Volume 14) (pbk)
ISBN: 978-1-315-44584-7 (Volume 14) (ebk)

Publisher's Note
The publisher has gone to great lengths to ensure the quality of this reprint but points out that some imperfections in the original copies may be apparent.

Disclaimer
The publisher has made every effort to trace copyright holders and would welcome correspondence from those they have been unable to trace.

GEORG KERSCHENSTEINER   from an etching by Oskar Graf

DIANE SIMONS

Georg Kerschensteiner

His thought and its relevance today

METHUEN & CO LTD
11 NEW FETTER LANE · LONDON EC4

© 1966 by Diane Simons
First published 1966 by Methuen & Co Ltd
Printed in Great Britain by
Richard Clay (The Chaucer Press) Ltd, Bungay, Suffolk

ACKNOWLEDGEMENTS

I should like to thank the librarians of the following libraries in this country who have assisted me in the acquisition of books: Harris Library, Preston, Leyland Library, School of Education Library, Manchester, Institute of Education Library, London, German Institute Library, London, Department of Education and Science Library, London. I should also like to express my sincere thanks to those headmasters and teachers in German vocational and technical schools who have shown such willingness to inform and discuss. To Professor Dobinson, for his constant kindness and encouragement, I shall always be grateful.

D. S.

The frontispiece portrait is reproduced from *Georg Kerschensteiner, Lebensweg eines Schulreformers* by Marie Kerschensteiner, by permission of the publishers R. Oldenbourg Verlag, Munich. The table of gross national products on p. 103 is taken from *The Times*, 29 September 1964.

Contents

1 EARLY LIFE 1
Childhood · Kerschensteiner the teacher · A student once more · A teacher again · Aims put into practice · Frustrations and opportunities

2 DIRECTOR OF EDUCATION 13
The first steps · The development of vocational school education in Germany · The situation confronting Kerschensteiner · Faults of the system

3 EDUCATION AND CITIZENSHIP 25
Factors which determine the path of education · Educational aims · Misunderstandings again · Education and work · The prize essay · Kerschensteiner's theories and the continuation schools

4 CHARACTER TRAINING 39
Interest · Altruism · The concept of character · The 'activity school' · The educative value of practical work

5 THE ORGANIZATION OF THE SCHOOLS 52
A broad basis for trade instruction · Altruism and civics · Group work · Other applications of group work · Responsibility · What form shall work take?

6 THE REALIZATION OF HIS PLANS 68
The beginnings · Foreign achievements · The reaction to his proposals · Linking the schools with industry · Details of the organization of the new schools · A reform of art teaching · The value of the sciences · The spread of his ideas · The education of girls · The education of rural youth

7 THE MODERN GERMAN VOCATIONAL SCHOOLS 87

The post-war situation · Civic teaching · The industrial and trades vocational schools · The commercial vocational schools · The domestic vocational schools · Agricultural vocational schools · Conclusion

8 FURTHER TECHNICAL EDUCATION IN MODERN GERMANY 105

Kerschensteiner's voluntary classes · Pre-occupational training · Technical schools · Technician schools · Higher technical schools · Further training in commerce · Commercial pre-occupational schools · Higher commercial schools · The economics high school · Schools for housekeeping · Technical schools for women's professions · Further education in agriculture · 'The alternative way'

9 INTO THE FUTURE 120

The lost opportunities · The course of technical education in England · Selection and efficiency · Economic trends and technical training · Folk High Schools · Kerschensteiner's philosophical studies · The cultural heritage and education · Kerschensteiner's validity today · Compulsory further education

NOTES 139

INDEX 149

1 · Early Life

CHILDHOOD

Georg Kerschensteiner was born in 1854 in Munich during a cholera epidemic. His family was poor and humble, for his father, originally of wealthy country stock, had lost almost all his means in various financial undertakings. Anton, his father, was fifty-one when he took as his second wife young Katherina, then a mere girl of nineteen, who showed him an almost filial love and devotion.

During the first years of their marriage they lived miserably in a small, dark, gloomy house in Munich. Anton was pitifully aware of their wretched financial situation, and tortured himself with self reproach for his weakness and inability to find some kind of employment whereby he could support his family. He was a firm upholder of the principles of truth, steadfastness, and justice, a severe man of quick and fiery temper, a man so strict in his manner than he seemed incapable of expressing his feelings. Katherina, on the other hand, was patient and tolerant, a pillar of affection and understanding for her husband and children, full of energy and exuberance, always willing and eager to take on any kind of work which would provide extra money for the family. Anton himself was not physically strong enough to take on manual work and so, in those first years, Katherina was often the breadwinner. Eventually, Anton was able to obtain a post as a parliamentary messenger.

Georg spent his boyhood days playing and romping down by the banks of the Isar River. His family had moved to a house near the Isar Gate and had taken over a small cheese shop as soon as their poverty had begun to recede. Life afforded many interests to a young boy not yet attending school, for when he was not playing at Indians or getting into some kind of scrape he would be watching all the interesting things and people in the market, or the sailors on the Isar, or the tradesmen going into Munich. He started school at the age of six, but, used to an active outdoor life, sat fidgety and inattentive in class – until on one particular occasion the despairing teacher offered a bribe by promising him a prize if he could manage to sit still for three whole days – which Georg promptly did. At home he had to be less boisterous, for his father was a strict disciplinarian who insisted above all on three things: obedience, order, and punctuality. Shoes had to be polished and brought for inspection, homework had to be done neatly and well, and help had to be given in the shop. When Georg was eight years old his parents sent him to have drawing lessons on Wednesday and Saturday afternoons: this proved to be the commencement of a hobby, interest in which was later to inspire him to reform the teaching of art in the Munich elementary schools.

In addition to active, outdoor pursuits Georg was passionately fond of reading; his family was, of course, too poor to buy books, so most of his literary experience came from the *Leipziger Allgemeine Zeitung*, which was kept for use as wrapping paper in the shop. More often than not he failed to understand or appreciate the style and import of what he read, but when he did understand some part he would jump for joy and strut around proudly reciting. The Kerschensteiner family had firm Catholic roots and Sunday was a day set apart from the other days of the week: attendance at church and gospel reading formed an integral part of the Sunday routine.

So his earliest youth passed by, until the fateful day arrived when he had to leave school and go out into the world. Georg was glad to leave school, but, when the hour finally arrived, he was beset by the great problem of what employment to take up. His parents, although without money to pay for extensive training, earnestly desired him to take up some kind of employment which would assure him a certain level of economic and social security, so that he would be spared the horrors of bankruptcy which they themselves had suffered. Knowing little about what prospects were open to a young lad of twelve or thirteen, who in class was neither particularly bright nor particularly dull, they sought advice from a friend of the family, Dr Rampf, later Bishop of Passau. After due consideration, Dr Rampf suggested that Georg should take up the priesthood – an idea which delighted both Georg's parents and Georg himself, who had always held priests and policemen in high esteem. The matter seemed settled when Georg, on discovering that the training would last twelve years, decided to weigh things up again, and then abandoned the idea in favour of something less complicated. His brother Josef immediately stepped in to try to save the situation by offering to find him a job in a shop in Cologne, but Georg flatly refused this post too, for this would mean his spending five years as an apprentice, plus several years as a journeyman. However, schooldays were nearing their end and a decision of some kind had to be made. So Georg chose the only path he could think of which demanded a comparatively short period of training – he would become a teacher.

Then followed a period of several years as a student at a teachers' seminary in Freising, near Munich, where Kerschensteiner led a spartan existence, regularly begging his mid-day meal from a kindly family in the town. The curriculum covered a large range of subjects which were both taught and learned mechanically: the pupils became passive recipients of knowledge, and were not trained at all to think for themselves nor to try to gain an insight into the deeper meaning or significance of what they learned. It is interesting to take a look at the subjects which Kerschensteiner studied during his period of teacher training: church history; biblical history; religion; universal history; physical, mathematical, and political geography; history of German literature; German composition; German grammar; arithmetic; algebra; planimetry; stereometry; writing; freehand drawing; linear drawing; mechanical drawing; general pedagogy; theory of instruction; psychology; zoology; botany; mineralogy with geology; chemistry; physics; human anatomy and physiology; piano; organ; violin; singing; harmony; cultivation of fruit trees; vestry accounts; church service; the system, method, and technique of gymnastics. Kerschensteiner hated all this rote learning and reciting which they were forced to do, and gradually, with the maturing of his mind and spirit, he came to reject this mode of learning and desired only active creative methods of acquiring knowledge.

There is an amusing story which illustrates his growing preoccupation with creative work. On one occasion he was very anxious to compose an andante, but had neither time nor solitude for composition, since he was fully employed in seminary studies. The only way of gaining the necessary freedom was by feigning sickness and being put in the sick-bay. However, after nearly two days of near starvation-level diet in the sick-bay, Kerschensteiner, desperate for a good meal, arranged for a fellow student to attach sausages to a piece of string which Kerschensteiner would then haul up to his window. Unfortunately, the sausages became entangled in the geraniums in the Präfekt's window-box on the floor below, and refused to budge. The andante was never mentioned again.

The school work aroused in him no interest at all, neither did the teachers, apart from one, named Dresely. This man stood apart from all the others, as a kind of Pestalozzi[1] who taught through love and understanding and approached his pupils with directness and personal interest – qualities which were to play a major role in Kerschensteiner's own theory and practice of education. Finally, the eagerly awaited day of freedom arrived, when he was to be loosened from the fetters of memorization and vain recitation and was to leave the doors of the seminary closed behind him for the last time.

KERSCHENSTEINER THE TEACHER

At the age of seventeen, Kerschensteiner entered the teaching profession on 17 September 1871 as an 'assistant' in a tiny village some fifteen miles east of Munich. Freedom had come at last, yet he was still fated to walk with those two unwelcome companions, disappointment and frustration, constantly beside him. His pupils, children of farmers and peasants, all cultivated a strong dislike and belligerent attitude both to school work and to any authority which represented it. They were resentful of scolding and paid no attention at all during lessons, seeking every excuse to stay away from school, especially in the summer months when there was work to be done in the fields. When there was no legitimate excuse for absence they simply played truant. Kerschensteiner was sorely taxed and hated the whole atmosphere in school; but it was not only at school that he felt dejected, for in this forsaken Bavarian village he was shut off from all cultural and intellectual life. His desire to read and learn was continually increasing, yet he had no money to buy books, and there was nobody of his own age and interests with whom he could have intellectual discussions. He felt thwarted in every direction. After a year of effort he managed to get himself posted to a suburb of Augsburg, and six months later to Augsburg itself. This was like a heaven-sent opportunity to him,

Early Life · 5

for amid all the intellectual and cultural hubbub of the city he had opportunity to fulfil his desire for more knowledge and experience of life.

He now had a passion for learning new things, but amid the satisfactions of Augsburg he also first experienced the frustration which so often accompanies the joy of learning. The more he learned, the more he became aware how abysmally ignorant and puny he was; but this made him more determined than ever to accept the challenge which life put before him. He and several similarly thinking colleagues decided to form a small study circle where one of the group would open a discussion on some prearranged topic at each meeting. Kerschensteiner was thrilled at the prospect of the intellectual stimulus which this society would offer and eagerly awaited his turn to address the meeting. His subject was to be a certain aspect of chemistry. Unfortunately, in his presentation he unconsciously applied the methods which he had learnt in the teachers' seminary and gave his talk in such a dry, stilted manner and introduced so much memorized material that, by the time he had finished, all his colleagues had dropped off to sleep. Kerschensteiner was utterly dejected and came to realize more and more the disparity between his aims and his actual achievements. Yet, despite these moments of despair and mental self-torment at his failure to reach the high standards which he had set himself, his desire to fight and his thirst for knowledge became so strong that he finally took the decision to pursue his studies further in a Gymnasium.[2]

A STUDENT ONCE MORE

In December 1873 he gave up his post, for he realized that it would not be possible for him both to study and to teach at the same time: the earnings from private lessons which he might give would help finance him. In 1875, when he was nearly twenty-one years old and had studied for almost two years, at first on his own, and then under teachers, he finally passed the examination which qualified him to enter the Sixth Form of the Gymnasium. During the following years at school his inquiring mind was never at rest: he was always urging himself on to more difficult tasks, challenging his ability and potential in all fields of study. The sciences attracted him greatly, and mathematics in particular, because it fulfilled his demands of the process of learning: namely, it demanded a brain which always worked at its top capacity, it demanded logical thinking, clarity of expression, and strict mental discipline. These two years at the top of the academic Gymnasium were most important for Kerschensteiner's inner development; they formed a period of self-discovery in which he evaluated his own powers and limitations, in which he came to terms with himself and with life. By the time he left school, now twenty-three years of age, he had formulated the ambition, which was long to hover before him – that he would be the best teacher in the best school in the most exact subject. We have the picture of a young man of great seriousness and intensity.

After the successful completion of his Gymnasium studies in 1877 Kerschensteiner became a student of mathematics and physics in Munich. Every minute of the day he was fully active, learning, seeing, and experiencing. It was a mark of his character that he was satisfied only with results which had been gained after intense exertion, and accordingly, he set himself intellectual tasks which could be achieved only by an almost superhuman effort. Consequently, he sometimes failed to achieve the tasks and high standards which he had imposed on himself, despite the enormous amount of energy and work which he directed on to his studies. But setbacks like these only made him more determined to take on the challenge. He had a Faustian yearning to gain universal experience and to embrace all spheres of knowledge. With the academic freedom, so well established in the German university system, it was possible to attend lectures on any subject outside one's own special field of study, and Kerschensteiner eagerly followed up any line of investigation which afforded him interest. These student years of 'Storm and Stress' were a time of continued mental and spiritual development, a period when his life was characterized by initiative, immense activity, and a struggling to attain those high ideals which he had formulated: a period of abundant joys and hopes, disappointments and sorrows. He felt great pride and pleasure at being able to study under Felix Klein, Germany's greatest mathematician, but, as always, his joy was qualified, for Klein insisted that his students devote their time and energy to mathematics alone – an idea which found Kerschensteiner's strong disapproval, for his zest for life penetrated far beyond the narrow confines of his special subject.

Kerschensteiner had become an enthusiastic member of the Munich mathematical society, founded by Max Planck,[3] and for two and a half years he was its president. He was also a keen artist, and always had his sketch-book with him when on excursions in the surrounding countryside. He was good at sports, a keen walker and mountaineer, and during the winter he often went on ski-ing expeditions into the Bavarian Alps. Music held a special place in his heart too, and he practised the piano every morning before beginning his work. He was an opera enthusiast and had a passionate admiration for Wagner in particular, who seemed to combine so many Germanic qualities in his works. Bismarck also came very high in his list of esteemed personalities, for Kerschensteiner was a fervent patriot and held honour and loyalty to one's country as two of the leading principles in his life. Throughout his days he always retained a deep loyalty and love for his own native Bavaria, for 'die schöne Heimat'.

His student days were hard in many ways, for there were struggles both on intellectual and financial planes. He was financed partly by the funds which were yielded by his mother's sausage stall (his father had died in 1877) and partly by the money he earned himself by giving private lessons. But despite all the struggles, Kerschensteiner was happy, for he enjoyed pitting his wits against the numerous problems which he came up against, and came to realize that happiness lay not in achievement itself but in the fight for achievement. At times he was beset by spiritual doubts too, for although he had received a sound Catholic upbringing he was beginning to question certain aspects of the faith. His fiancée, an Augsburg girl, was of great comfort to him in these moments of indecision, for she had a fervent and instinctive belief in the principles of Roman Catholicism and Kerschensteiner could always rely on her inexhaustible love to furnish him with fresh energy with which he could come to terms with life.

After graduation Kerschensteiner, aged twenty-seven, undertook a special study for one year, when, in order to be able to remain in Munich and to pursue his work at the university, he accepted a post at the meteorological office in Munich, from which the salary now enabled him to support his mother. The work was uninteresting – the only departure from dull routine being when Kerschensteiner used to attach a slight tail to the figure 7 on the meteorological reports which were posted up in the town of Augsburg, where his bride-to-be would eagerly watch for the notice and count the number of tails, which represented the number of 'Greetings' which Kerschensteiner sent her. In July 1883 he obtained his doctorate, for work on theories of electricity, and in the autumn of the same year, at the age of twenty-nine, he became a teacher once more – twelve years after taking up his first post in the teaching profession.

A TEACHER AGAIN

His appointment in 1883 was as assistant teacher for mathematics at the Melanchthon Gymnasium in Dürer's town of Nürnberg. His attitude towards teaching had matured considerably during his years of study and intercourse with people; his greatest desire now was not merely to give instruction but to do all within his power to help the youngsters develop an active mind and, through his own enthusiasm, to pass on some of his own overflowing zest for life. He was passionately interested in the personal and human aspects of teaching, for his wide experience of people of all ranks and ages in the last few years had shown him that, however humble the background or low the intelligence, there was something good in all men. He saw that it was the job of the teacher to find this goodness, in whatever form it expressed itself, and to tend it as a plant and so bring it to full bloom. He realized that this would be best effected when the personal contact between pupil and teacher was so close that each had complete trust and confidence in the other and both were bound together by honesty and good will. Kerschensteiner had studied no pedagogy at university and had now forgotten what psychology he had memorized in long lists at the seminary. In fact, in his teaching he used no psychology at all as such; the 'method' which he desired to apply was a self-discovered one, one that grew from instinct and could not be analysed. He desired to approach his pupils through love, or, in measured terms, through personal regard.

When he took up his post, however, he was due for a rude awakening, for the relationship between pupils and staff was anything but friendly, and there was no possibility of approaching the pupils on friendly terms during class time, since, by tradition, the teachers taught and the pupils learned – and there was the end of it.

Yet, far from being downcast at this state of affairs, Kerschensteiner willingly accepted the challenge and demanded even more effort from himself. He saw that he could win over the pupils in out-of-school time, and accordingly took up sports in the afternoons or went

Early Life · 9

swimming with them. The pupils were amazed that a teacher should give up his spare time for their activities, and more so, that he should really enjoy being with them, as Kerschensteiner so obviously did. Everything they did, they did together, until gradually a community feeling grew among them and Kerschensteiner was regarded as being one of them. In time, his honest directness and openness towards them was reciprocated, and Kerschensteiner began to see what a one-sided view of the pupil the classroom gave, for those who were either dull or lazy in class showed other positive traits when out on the sports field or when engaged in general conversation. Kerschensteiner became very popular in school and often was looked on by the pupils as a 'Kamerad' – someone in whom they could confide on serious matters, and someone with whom they could also have 'fun'. During lesson time Kerschensteiner tried to retain this personal link with his pupils and taught as much as possible without textbooks, for he still remembered with horror his years at the seminary. His lessons were based, to a large extent, on concrete, everyday objects within the child's experience: his mathematics lessons would incorporate such work as the detailed costs of building a house, or calculating the costs of running a home. He always endeavoured to bring his sense of humour into the classroom too. But woe betide any child who deserved punishment, for Kerschensteiner had inherited some of his father's severity and fiery temper.

In addition to teaching he also travelled from Nürnberg to Erlangen university every week, a distance of some fourteen miles, in order to join a group of workers led by Professor Gordan, who later asked Kerschensteiner to compile and publish his lecture notes. Kerschensteiner was overjoyed at the prospect of this work, but the strain of the now almost daily trips to Erlangen, which the work necessitated, combined with the industrial air of Nürnberg was detrimental to his health; he published two volumes of the work[4] and finally abandoned the huge task.

In 1885 he took up a post as mathematics master at the commercial school in Nürnberg. He had enjoyed his work at the state school, but the post at the commercial school, a school controlled by the town authorities, carried with it a higher salary, so that he would now, at last, be able to marry; the marriage took place in 1886. However, his new post too, brought him many disappointments, for the standard of teaching and level of achievement were mediocre, the teachers too easily satisfied with their work and teaching methods, and all opposed any change in the system. During this period in Nürnberg Kerschensteiner had continued to keep up his sketching and also took a very active part in the musical life of the town, as well as being an enthusiastic member of any discussion groups. Unfortunately, his wife, who had previously led a quiet life, was rather uneasy among company and often did not participate in Kerschensteiner's busy social life.

AIMS PUT INTO PRACTICE

In September 1890 he moved to Schweinfurt, where he was appointed teacher at the Gustav-Adolf Gymnasium. This was a most significant phase in his career, for it was here that he was really able to put into practice those thoughts and methods which had been occupying his mind for so long. Shortly after his arrival there, the headmaster asked him to take on the teaching of nature study in the lower school; but Kerschensteiner had never undertaken a detailed study of botany or zoology and refused to take on a task unless he knew that he could do it well. The headmaster was amazed at Kerschensteiner's reluctance, for the teacher who had previously taught the subject had also received no specific training for it, but had simply followed the set syllabus. This, Kerschensteiner absolutely refused to do: the headmaster finally gave in and Kerschensteiner decided to attend lectures twice a week in Würzburg, so that he would feel qualified to teach the subject later, should he be required to do so. He also joined the natural history club in Schweinfurt, which became for him a substitute for the various music circles in Nürnberg, for through the club he met many interesting people from all professions, from whom he could receive intellectual stimulus.

He became fascinated by the discovery of the local flora and fauna and was an eager participant in all the excursions which the club arranged. A year later Kerschensteiner took over the botany teaching in the lower part of the school and was delighted with the response from his pupils. He never allowed the basis of his lessons to be explanations or theories: specimens were drawn and examined with minute care and attention. Kerschensteiner regularly took the whole class out into the woods and fields where they could observe the plants in their natural setting. The pupils were overjoyed at this new practical method

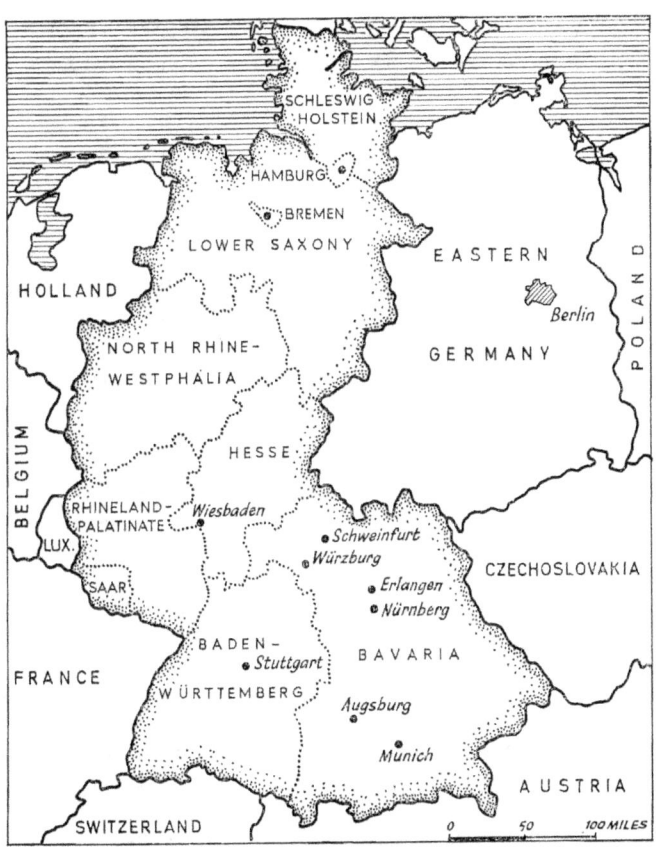

WESTERN GERMANY

of learning and, while they were very pleased with their new teacher, who taught them through his own interest and enthusiasm, Kerschensteiner in turn was overjoyed at the interest which they showed. 'It's like dried-up soil greedily sipping the first rain,' he wrote in a letter to Ludwig Schleiermacher.[5] It was in Schweinfurt that Kerschensteiner developed a strong passion for nature study: he took immense care in the observation, drawing, and annotation of specimens, and several times in the following years took part in glacier surveys in the Central Alps.

FRUSTRATIONS AND OPPORTUNITIES

Three years later, in Autumn 1893, he came back again to his beloved Munich, to be teacher of mathematics and physics in the upper school of the Ludwigs Gymnasium. Eager, too, to keep up his newly found interest in nature study, he voluntarily taught nature study in the lower school. Although he was delighted at the prospect of living in the intellectual atmosphere in Munich again, he was once more disappointed in both staff and pupils at his new school, for the school's traditional role was that of imparting knowledge and nothing more. He also found that he could no longer do justice to his botany teaching because of the lack of interest among the pupils of a large city and the impossibility of obtaining specimens near at hand. He did succeed, however, in organizing many day and week-end trips both into the surrounding districts and to the lakes in the South – trips which were greatly enjoyed by all the participants.

Yet, however bad the school situation seemed, he always tried to live by his motto: 'Take things as they come and yet make the best of them.' His financial situation was still not satisfactory and after school hours he was giving private lessons to help out his salary, for by now he had three children, and living costs in Munich were high. It was a period when there seemed little opportunity available to him to employ his energy and efforts in the solution of the difficult and worthwhile tasks which he demanded of himself. In the past he had always had great aims and ambitions for helping people, and had always entertained hopes that they would be realised in the future: the future had lain open and challenging before him. Now he was forty, had fallen short of his hopes, and the future no longer held the same positive attraction. His inquiring mind was still too active for his restricted situation; his desire was not for rest but for problems and circumstances which would tax all his mental and spiritual resources. He was a man of immense will-power and determination. He wanted to approach his pupils through the only way he knew – through personal regard – but what could he do, an isolated voice crying out in the wilderness of dry academics? Never, it seemed to him, had the future held so little hope for him.

Then suddenly and unexpectedly an opportunity, one of which he had never dreamed, was given him, which would fulfil all his desires and longings. The post of Director of Education of Munich[6] had become vacant and had been offered to Dr Niklas, a protestant. So much criticism had, however, been raised in this catholic town against this important post having been offered to a protestant, that poor Dr Niklas had felt morally obliged to decline the offer. He was made head of the humanistic Gymnasium as compensation, and Kerschensteiner, whom Dr Niklas himself had recommended, obtained the post at the head of the Munich school system. This meant that Kerschensteiner was virtually in control of the organization of the entire Munich school system.

2 · Director of Education

THE FIRST STEPS

Kerschensteiner was overjoyed at the news of his appointment to this important post, an appointment in which the helping hand of chance was to be discerned. Up till now he had been employed as a mere tool in the academic school system, caught up in the web of mechanical learning, recitation, and bookish study. He had fought against the system as far as he had been able, and had introduced a spontaneous vitality into his own lessons, so that his own pupils were no longer passive recipients of a collection of facts and data, but were actively and creatively involved in the eager acquisition of new knowledge. Yet, however great his efforts had been, Kerschensteiner's beneficial and refreshing influence had never extended beyond the walls of his own school, for he had found far too little support among his colleagues. There were few in the teaching profession who fought, as he had done, to free themselves from the imprisoning fetters in educational methods and to curb the respected esteem for theory and vain knowledge.

Now, with the announcement of his appointment, Kerschensteiner's prospects were suddenly reversed, and the future lay open and inviting before him. No longer was he one of the many, an insignificant member of the teaching profession, but was suddenly transported to much loftier planes, and found himself seated on the throne of the Munich educational system, with the eyes of all Munich pivoted upon him. True, not all the eyes betrayed hopeful expectancy and approval: many critics poured sarcasm on the appointment of this 'village schoolmaster' to the direction of Munich's schools. Kerschensteiner was not deterred, however, for his past experience had shown him that his determination and zeal grew best on the ground where criticism was at its strongest. He was willing and prepared to carry on his fight in the face of all adversity, and this, although he did not know it at the time, was exactly what he would have to do for many years to come.

Kerschensteiner's first test in the eyes of his critics came when he delivered his inaugural speech, in which he outlined what he considered to be the main aims and tasks of the elementary schools (Volksschulen), which were the schools attended by the vast majority of schoolchildren. Kerschensteiner said that the schools should aim at imparting clear and simple knowledge and skills, at strengthening the body and improving bodily dexterity, at awakening a deep and inner feeling for what is pure, good, and beautiful, and at strengthening the pupils' will towards work and morality. In order that the child should be led towards the Good, his education should be imparted on a firm religious foundation; new knowledge and skills were to be acquired by studying a limited amount of material with a deeper penetration into the subject matter; bodily strength and dexterity were to be improved through regular lessons in sports, gymnastics, and crafts, and the will was to be strengthened by all three of these methods.

This inaugural speech made enemies for Kerschensteiner all over Munich: very few of them had actually been present when the speech had been given, but all Bavaria read the critical reports in the Munich papers, which published bitter attacks both on his speech and on his appointment. Right from the very beginning of his career in educational administration Kerschensteiner stood apart, with few supporters, flanked on all sides by contempt and criticism. He had scarcely had time to settle down in his new office when his first gigantic task was set before him. An urgent request was made to him by the local teachers to revise the curriculum in the elementary schools. Kerschensteiner now heard again from these teachers the very same criticism and shouts of despair, which he himself had uttered so many times during his teaching career, against the huge amount of subject matter and unnecessary knowledge which was being taught.

The mammoth task of familiarizing himself with the curricula and teaching methods in the elementary schools now lay before him, and Kerschensteiner frequently worked well on into the early hours of the morning, poring over official reports and textbooks dealing with teaching methods, so as to gain a good foundation for his practical investigations. Then followed a year of visiting first one school and then another, having consultations with pupils and teachers, listening to their views and criticism, sitting in at lessons, observing methods and aims, examining school buildings and equipment. After three years in the post his investigations were at last complete, and he was able to produce his plans for alteration and improvement. His views on the principles to be considered in the organization of the curriculum were published in his *Considerations on the Curriculum* in 1899.[1] The new proposals found wide approval among the inspectorate, but aroused opposition among the general public and in the ranks of the elementary school teachers.

During his extensive investigations he had found both pupils and teachers to be, on the whole, satisfactory, but had seen too many examples of old-fashioned methods and inadequate equipment. He ascertained that the two main teaching methods in elementary school education, the Kehr and Rein-Pickel methods, both led to sheer mechanical learning and gave no opportunity for the children's minds to develop and expand, since no active or creative thought ever accompanied the learning process. In his report, Kerschensteiner attached great importance to the principles that the pupil should only be taught that knowledge which was useful and necessary to him, and that all that he was taught at school should come within the realm of his experience. Only too often had he seen youngsters struggling against the huge amount of knowledge which was thrust at them, and which, in all likelihood, they would never need in their later lives. He stressed, also, that the subjects in the curriculum should be related to each other as far as possible, so that the teaching formed a unity and the child became aware of the bonds which connect all subjects and all aspects of life. The mind, too, should be trained in such a way as to follow the principle of what Kerschensteiner called 'economy of thought', that is, a process whereby the mind became accustomed to drawing its thoughts together and grouping them under different headings, and then arranging these headings in such a way that the final goal was reached – a comprehension of the pattern of the world and of the harmonious forces, all working together in it to form a unity. These principles which guided the new plans for the organization of the elementary schools were principles which had emerged from his own teaching experience and from the careful thought and reflection he had given over the years. The reforms aroused cutting attacks from various quarters and persisted for many months.

Yet, although it was in the field of elementary school education that Kerschensteiner made his administrative début, his fame and acclaim were to come as a result of his inspiring and revolutionary work in quite a different aspect of education. It was, namely, in the realm of vocational education that he was to achieve renown and to make what came to be called the 'Munich system' famous not only throughout Germany but throughout the whole of Europe.

THE DEVELOPMENT OF VOCATIONAL SCHOOL EDUCATION IN GERMANY

With the development and extended use of the printing press, which Johann Gutenberg had invented in 1445, Luther's revolutionary ideas had penetrated into all corners of Germany. He was the first great German thinker to occupy himself with education and to demand a system of compulsory education for all – boys and girls alike. He proposed that, in addition to giving a religious training, it should be the job of the schools to give their pupils a solid foundation in the skills, accomplishments and knowledge which they would require in their everyday life as workers, heads of families, and citizens, and that the curriculum of existing schools should be extended accordingly. He placed considerable emphasis on the child learning the skills of his trade, which was to be the basis of his future livelihood. During this period the first Sunday schools were set up in Württemberg (they were first mentioned in documents in 1559)[2] and were attended by children who had already completed their elementary school education. The purpose of these schools was to ensure that their pupils retained the knowledge and skills which they had acquired in the elementary schools and continued to receive a religious and moral education.

For more than a hundred and fifty years these schools continued to be introduced all over Württemberg and in other states, and in 1739 it was again Württemberg which took the initiative and introduced compulsory attendance at them. ('All young people must attend Sunday school until they marry, so that they do not easily forget what they have learned in the elementary school.'[3]) In the same regulations, less emphasis was placed on religious instruction and more on the teaching of general subjects. This broadening of the curriculum found wide approval not only within the boundaries of Württemberg itself but also throughout the whole of Germany, with the result that similar schools were introduced in many of the German states during the course of the next decades. By the end of the eighteenth century Sunday schools had become widespread over vast areas of Germany, and, more and more, the curriculum tended not only to revise elementary school work but also to supplement and extend it.

At the time when interest was being aroused in the Sunday school movement, the need for elementary school education for *all* was beginning to be felt. The broader aspects of education had been avidly discussed since Comenius, who had died in 1670, had put forward his theory that man was a creature who should be *trained*, and that the opportunity of receiving this training should be given to all men, whatever their status in life. The first compulsory attendance laws had already been enacted in 1619 in the state of Weimar, and during the seventeenth and eighteenth centuries elementary schools were founded all over Germany and compulsory attendance introduced.

At the same time, there was a move to broaden the school curriculum and to introduce those subjects which would prove useful to the child in later life. Comenius, too, had already pointed the way to the introduction of crafts in schools. At the beginning of the eighteenth century, the first of the new Realschulen were founded by the Pietists, under the leadership of Francke.[4] The new feature of these schools was that, besides preparing their pupils spiritually for the after-life, they also devoted much of their energy to giving them the knowledge necessary for this life. A study of the mother tongue, history, geography, mathematics, practical work, French, and nature study all found ready acceptance in these schools, which found great support in Prussia especially. During the same period Prussia was occupying herself with the problem of elementary school education too, at which compulsory attendance was imposed in 1763 for all youngsters between the ages of five to twelve or thirteen.

Since the end of the religious struggles, the importance of worldly aspects of everyday life had risen to the fore and attention was focused increasingly on the acquisition of material gains and personal happiness. The discovery and application of new facts and skills had brought greater comfort and efficiency both in the home and at work, so that, gradually, the need became apparent for workers who had been trained in new methods, who would be able to cope with the sudden increase in trade and commerce. By the end of the seventeenth century it had become imperative for higher personnel and business proprietors to undergo some kind of special training in their trade, so that they could deal with the new expanding economic situation. Accordingly, several specialized technical schools came into existence. During the eighteenth century there arose a great enthusiasm for these schools, which were attended by the prospering middle classes and were to train their students for the higher positions in the various trades. They gave a sound and thorough professional training to those who held important posts in all spheres of economic and artistic life – schools of mining, building, commerce, shipbuilding, textiles, and a host of other trades suddenly sprang into life, and continued to be founded throughout the nineteenth century, when they were supplemented by the new technical universities which were emerging (Karlsruhe, 1825; Munich, 1827; Hannover, 1828; etc.).

For the bourgeoisie the end of the eighteenth century was characterized by the spirit of classicism, idealism, and humanism. Intellectuals were preoccupied with a study of Antiquity and the ideals which they found there: the value of the individual and his harmonious personality, the nobility of man and the greatness to which he can aspire, his spiritual, mental, and physical perfection. And so, from the ranks of the middle classes there emerged a genuine desire to improve the lot of the working masses, and to give them an education above and beyond that offered by the ordinary elementary school. In time, various wealthy individuals and societies took upon themselves to found a new type of school, which would be made available to the working classes for their further education.

These schools, called trade schools, proved to be a tremendous success and soon spread all over Germany, initiated, for the main part, by the prospering middle classes. They held their classes on Sundays, and, although they were named trade schools, they really gave very little technical education, taking their teachers from the church and secondary schools, and experienced workers from the individual trades. The significant part which these schools had to play in the economic development of the country was quickly appreciated, and North and Central Germany in particular forged ahead with their introduction. On the whole, East and South Germany preferred the old type of Sunday school, yet at the same time, the importance of the trade schools was not to be underestimated, so much so, that in 1836 Württemberg, for instance, passed a law to the effect that the compulsory school attendance on a Sunday could, from then on, be fulfilled either at the religious Sunday school or at the Sunday trade school.

The trade schools reached the height of their popularity at the end of the Napoleonic Wars, when the demand for skilled and well-trained workers was at its greatest. The Germans became increasingly aware of the fact that a successful economy was based on efficient and skilled workers who could apply new and quick methods of production, and in the immediate post-war years it was these thoughts, rather then the original humanitarian principle, which inspired the foundation of further Sunday trade schools. The success of these schools can best be shown from the figures: in 1818 Württemberg, for instance, had eleven trade schools; by 1846 she had over seventy. Most of the trade schools throughout Germany offered a similar type of education, but already some states were looking ahead to a Germany which was becoming characterized by increasing trade specialization and were already planning their education to meet the needs of the future society. The Ministry of Education in the state of Baden was particularly forward looking in this question, for instance, and stressed the teaching of technical subjects in its trade schools. Lessons were also moved from Sundays to weekdays and the schools had to be attended for at least six hours per week, for between two to three years.

Towards the middle of the nineteenth century, similar movements in the reorganization of the trade schools took place in other parts of Germany. Lessons were moved to weekdays and the subject matter was extended to include both more general and technical subjects. Gradually, the trade schools came to be attended by the more gifted pupils and were centred only on the towns. Because of this elevation of status of the trade schools, the ordinary Sunday schools, which had still continued to exist, now assumed a greater importance for the education of the ordinary worker.

Despite movements in different parts of the country to introduce more specialized and technical teaching in the schools, such as was being enforced with great vigour in Prussia, which previously had lagged behind in the whole field of further education, the prevailing literary and intellectual trends favoured by far a more general type of education. The main streams of German intellectual thought at this time concentrated not on professional training but turned towards Greece for their inspiration: man was to be ennobled and enriched through contact with the masterpieces of Antiquity, permeated with the spirit of 'noble simplicity and quiet greatness'. Technical and professional training could find no place in a philosophy such as this, which could approve only of a classical education. Thus, although the existing specialized technical schools continued to exist and even to flourish during this period, they were scorned by the influential middle classes, who saw them as possessing a purely utilitarian character and as having no *educational* value whatsoever. During the main part of the nineteenth century the split between those establishments offering professional training and those imparting the more traditional, general type of education became more pronounced, not least under the influence of Wilhelm von Humboldt[5] in Prussia and the ideas of pseudo-humanism which he represented.

Wilhelm von Humboldt had received wide acclaim throughout

Director of Education · 21

Germany for his sweeping reforms of the German university system. His views on the necessity that man should receive a broad and wide education found approval both among educationists and the solid middle classes. He maintained that a harmonious and balanced personality was to be acquired by the development and pursuit of the educand's varied talents and interests, and that vocational training gave a thoroughly narrow and biased view of life and should thus never be given an important place in the basic educational system. If vocational training must be given, then it should only be imparted *after* the broader general education.

THE SITUATION CONFRONTING KERSCHENSTEINER

These were, for the main part, the views which dominated the educational scene in the mid-nineteenth century, when the existing system of further education was undergoing constant criticism. The firm ranks of the bourgeoisie believed that it was the task of the schools to produce men who could converse easily and intelligently on a wide range of general subjects, men who had a close acquaintanceship with the classics in particular, men who were what they termed 'cultured' – and the successful education of these men could never be effected if they gave themselves up to a close preoccupation with vocational or technical subjects. This movement towards general education was so overpowering that it dragged along with it the system of further education for the workers. The workers, too, were to be given a general education.

By the 1870s, Germany had come to recognize that it was important that some kind of further, post-elementary school education, above and beyond the ordinary Sunday school system, should be given to *all* German youth, and, in the following decade, the heated debates as to the form it should take pointed continuously to the introduction of a *general* continuation school. The form of this type of school gained immediate approval all over the country, and almost at once numerous general continuation schools were formed in a wave of fervent enthusiasm. The Sunday schools had already been renamed continuation schools and now they came into line with the new system; gradually too, any school that had shown a leaning towards technical education came under the influence of the 'general education' movement, and put its curriculum on a much broader basis.

The new continuation schools had several features in common with the old Sunday schools, in as far as they both gave a firm religious and ethical basis to their instruction. But they were to make their curriculum more relevant to the needs of 1870 society: for example, the new school regulations in Saxony in 1873 stated, 'It is the job of the continuation schools to provide a further general education and especially to consolidate that knowledge and those skills which are of value in civic life.' In general, the curriculum devoted a large proportion of the teaching time to instruction in reading, writing, and arithmetic; additional subjects included nature study and the rudiments of political economy and constitutional law. The number of hours of lessons per week varied from state to state, but, on average, they were between six and eight, and were usually given in the evenings. The new general continuation schools remained very closely connected with the elementary schools from the organizational point of view, for they were usually housed in the same buildings, and very often it was the elementary school teachers who gave the instruction. This meant that it was quite possible for a pupil to leave the elementary school and to proceed to the general continuation school – only to be taught by the same teacher.

The new schools were a huge success and reaped special praise from private wealthy sponsors and humanitarian societies, who recognized the importance of giving further education to the workers, whose role in Bismarck's new economic state was not to be underestimated. The actual form of the schools, that is, as establishments which gave a *general* education, was found to be most satisfactory, and the schools remained in high esteem until the turn of the century, when Kerschensteiner and others were to point to a different direction in the training of German youth. The astounding initial success of these general continuation schools soon led to the introduction of compulsory attendance, although the individual states were by no means uniform in their regulations. Saxony, for instance, was one of the first to tackle the question, and in 1873 introduced compulsory attendance at general continuation schools: boys now had to attend them for a period of three years, and local authorities were empowered to introduce compulsory attendance for girls for two years. In the following year Baden and Hesse made attendance at continuation schools compulsory, and the other states quickly followed suit. The South was notably slower in the introduction of the new general continuation schools, and it was not until 1895 that Württemberg introduced compulsory attendance at the general continuation school, although some twenty-four years previously its local authorities had been empowered to enforce attendance in their area. Catholic Bavaria even preferred to retain the old Sunday school system, with its three years of compulsory attendance; however, although these were in name Sunday schools, their form bore a strong resemblance to that of the new general continuation school.

FAULTS OF THE SYSTEM

And so, before the end of the nineteenth century, all young Germans were attending courses of further education for two to three years after completion of their elementary school studies (generally at about the age of thirteen, although this varied from state to state) – or so it would seem: but, in reality, although tremendous progress had been made in this field in the last quarter of the nineteenth century, the regulations of the states insisted only on attendance at the schools already in existence – and there were no laws to the effect that schools must be established. Therefore, while it is true that the existing schools were being attended and that compulsory attendance was actually enforced in some towns, there remained vast country areas where there were neither buildings nor teachers to meet with the demand, and attendance could not be enforced.

During the first years in his new post, which he took up in 1895, Kerschensteiner had spent a great deal of time in making detailed investigations into all aspects of the educational system and had thus necessarily come into close contact with the work being achieved by the general continuation schools. In his visits to the continuation and Sunday schools, the point that impressed itself particularly on his mind was the fact that the proportion of knowledge which the pupils had retained from their elementary schools was absolutely minimal. The pupils also took very little interest in their further education. In general, the curriculum seemed to bear little relevance to the everyday life and pursuits of the pupils and was overburdened with subjects, so that the limited hours of teaching did not allow the pupils to study any one subject to a sufficient depth to gain a real and lasting benefit. In addition to this, the classes were held mainly in the evenings when the pupils were already tired after a full day's work and were unwilling, and even unable, to concentrate on their lessons.

The teachers, too, seemed indifferent to their task; classes were large, with a considerable range of intelligence in each class; little progress or continuity in subject matter was possible, because of the short amount of time devoted to each subject weekly. The youngsters received no encouragement from their employers, who regarded them as profitable underlings who should be kept to heel. In all, the position of the general continuation schools was a pitiable one, lacking both aim and sense of purpose.

Meanwhile Kerschensteiner was still under attack from some critics for his ideas on the reorganization of the elementary schools, and it seemed that there could be no end to the criticism levelled at him, until, suddenly, his critics were frozen into a respectful silence at the announcement of a piece of news which staggered all Bavaria. Out of seventy-nine competitors from all parts of the realm, the Royal Prussian Academy for Useful Knowledge had awarded the prize of their essay competition in 1900 to Georg Kerschensteiner, Director of Education in Munich. The subject of the competition, 'How is our youth best to be educated for citizenship, in the years between the completion of elementary education and conscription?' was one which had occupied Kerschensteiner's thoughts for many years, and he had eagerly seized the opportunity of setting his ideas down on paper. The age group mentioned in the essay was, of course, that of those pupils attending the general continuation school, and Kerschensteiner's plans for these schools, as set out in the essay, were to revolutionize the whole of educational thinking all over Germany. At last the opportunity for action had arrived – and Kerschensteiner was the man to undertake it.

3 · Education and Citizenship

FACTORS WHICH DETERMINE THE PATH OF EDUCATION

Both in his prize essay and in other later works, Kerschensteiner attached importance to the fact that it was not possible to consider properly the aims of education, without first considering the type of State and civilization in which the education was to be carried out; for the aims of education and their realization greatly depended both on the attitude of the State towards education, and on the role which it allotted its citizens in the State. The process and ideals of education were determined, to a large extent, by the social, political, and economic circumstances of that civilization in which the pupils were being educated, for in its educational system the State would always lay stress on the development of those particular qualities which it saw as being of value to it, at that particular stage of civilization. However great a civilization, its educational ideals would not necessarily be the same as those of a civilization equally as great; for example, both the Greeks and the Romans realized the *value* of education, yet their educational *aims* were different:

'Although the Romans took over almost all the essential elements of education from the Greeks, their aim in education differed fundamentally from that of the Greeks. For the Romans, education was a means to an end, a ladder to the high positions in the state, but for the Greeks, education was valuable for its own sake: it was the honour necessary to the true man. And so, for the truly great Greek thinkers and for her schools as well, the characteristic of the educated man was wisdom, φιλοσοφία, whereas for the Romans it was eloquence. . . . All in all, one could perhaps briefly define the aim of education of the Romans as being VIRTUS, proficiency related to the tasks of the statesman, and that of the Greeks, on the other hand, as being nobility of body and soul.'[1]

Kerschensteiner showed how, later on in the Middle Ages, church and state were alienated, and the church took control over all education in Germany, basing the teaching on preparation for the after-life. In the fifteenth and sixteenth centuries this spiritualism gave way to humanism, which emphasized the study of the ancient classics. Since the wars of liberation the element of nationalism had become stronger. From these examples Kerschensteiner intended to show that: 'An educational aim grows out of all the beliefs of a people and thus cannot be prescribed to any other people nor be taken over by another people.'[2]

He pointed out how the eighteenth- and nineteenth-century humanists in the age of enthusiasm and idealism had demanded the introduction of elementary schools, and how the ideas of Herbart[3] and Pestalozzi had subsequently found wide acceptance. By the close of the nineteenth century, when Kerschensteiner took up his new post in Munich, the elementary schools had become firmly established in Germany, attended by children aged between six to thirteen or fourteen years, but, unfortunately, these schools were bent on training the pupil in purely academic subjects and, in Kerschensteiner's view, the curriculum had become so crammed with material that none of it could be studied satisfactorily.

All these systems of education were reflections of life and policy in the past. What were to be the aims of existing and future schools? Kerschensteiner reflected how, at the beginning of the nineteenth century, when the German compulsory school system was still in its initial stage of enthusiasm and idealistic humanitarianism, and before it had become obsessed with the idea of cramming the heads of its pupils with knowledge of various kinds, the Bavarians had brought forward school directives which Kerschensteiner saw as still bearing a great deal of relevance to the requirements of society in his time. These directives of 1803 included the following points:

'Since there is an almost complete lack of useful education given in the home, educational establishments must be organized in such a way that through them the intellectual education of our youth, and especially its moral education, is furthered. Only in this way will they become what they really should be, namely, establishments whereby people are made capable of attaining their calling (Bestimmung).

'For every person this calling is a twofold one: a general and a special calling.

'The general calling of each person is the calling of *pure morality*; the special calling is that of *usefulness*, that is to say, that as a member of a civic society he must be put in the position to contribute as much as is possible to his own welfare and to the general welfare of the society in which he lives. Thus education is concerned with the *moral, intellectual,* and *technical* training of man.

'Moral education, pure morality, will only be reached through an overruling love for everything that is good and through a recognition of the Good. Neither of these will be obtained through the person becoming familiar with moral precepts and systems, nor through his learning the ethics and doctrine of religion off by heart, but they will be acquired if the person's moral feeling is awakened early on in life, and if he is imbued with principles which necessarily develop out of this feeling. These principles must then be consolidated by the tenets of religion, which show them to be the will of the Wisest Lawgiver and Kind Father. And so, religion is an essential part of the instruction; but the seed of the word of God falls upon unfruitful ground, if the real teaching is imparted not to the heart but to the memory.

'Man's intellectual training, too, must bring him nearer to his general calling of pure morality, otherwise this teaching would produce harmful knowledge. In addition to this, the instruction must take into account man's special calling; that is to say, it must make him *useful*.

'Certain technical skills are needed by more or less everyone, and, for this reason, it is imperative for trade schools (Arbeitsschulen) for boys and girls to be set up, which would work in collaboration with academic schools. All youngsters should attend these schools, including those who have no need to work for their living, for, apart from cases of change of circumstances, whereby many lose inherited wealth, it is always good for everyone to learn to appreciate the advantage of being able to earn his keep, and to pay due respect to the man who has learnt to acquire prosperity through industry and diligence.'[4]

These directives, with their emphasis on the need to train the pupils to be moral personalities and to be useful to the society in which they live, have much in common with Kerschensteiner's own views on the function of schools within the framework of modern society.

EDUCATIONAL AIMS

The aims of education were determined, as Kerschensteiner pointed out, by the form of the state in which that education was to be imparted, and the educational aims with which he himself was occupied were those that would also be acceptable to the ideal State. He did not devise an educational system intended for Germany, as it existed at the end of the nineteenth century, but conceived of one which would educate the members of a constitutional, democratic State, which was the State-form which he considered to be ideal. The aim of this ideal State and of all its education would be 'to produce a society consisting as far as possible of persons who had independence of mind, a harmonious development, and who were morally free'.[5] It would give its members as extended an education as possible, for this would be to the advantage of the democratic State, which was entirely dependent on its members for its own preservation and well-being.

The ideal education would not aim at developing any one faculty alone, but would concentrate rather on a development of the skills, knowledge, and virtues requisite of the 'citizen'. The citizen would have to be trained to perform useful work, which would bring both to him and to the State a certain material benefit; he must also have an understanding of the purpose and functions of the State, and he had to be a person whose deeds were governed by moral principles and who strongly supported the moral ideals upon which the State based its existence. Above all, the ideal citizen had to hold those moral principles in such high respect, that he realized his own self-fulfilment in serving both them and the continued progress of the State.

This theory of 'education for citizenship' placed Kerschensteiner among the pioneers of 'modern' education, for, according to his philosophy, the educand, the object of the educational process, was to become neither the nineteenth-century intellectual, nor the German classicists' perfect individual. Here was a complete break with traditional thinking, for Kerschensteiner's conception of the individual was that of a man who was essentially a social being, a member of a community, whose education would be such that it would aim at

Education and Citizenship · 29

equipping him to play his part as a member of that society. Just as the State put all its energy and efforts into providing for the preservation and continued welfare of itself and of the people who constituted it, so Kerschensteiner's system of education was to educate its members to form a community of thinking, selfless, efficient people all working willingly and joyfully together for the betterment and progress of the State. Neither would they be content to apply their skills and qualities of character merely in the pursuit of the State's economic or material progress, but would seek to apply them also in the pursuit of the ethical advancement of the State.

MISUNDERSTANDINGS AGAIN

Kerschensteiner's term 'education for citizenship' was widely abused during his own lifetime, for many critics maintained that this was by no means a new aspect in German education, but that it had already received considerable attention in discussions on school organization. This is true to a certain extent, for, by the end of the last century, a special awareness of the State had evolved and an enthusiasm for Teutonic qualities was an essential characteristic of the new Germans. The nineteenth-century absolutist rule had trained the Germans to be useful, efficient State servants and, by the 1890s, when Kerschensteiner's ideas were being put forward, this habit of subservience to the State had been supplemented by an awareness of Nietzsche's idealist superman cult, which was avidly seized upon by the countless disgruntled intellectuals who were being churned out of university only to find that they were a common commodity on the employment market.

Fichte's 'Addresses to the German Nation', written at the beginning of the nineteenth century, had now found a new and urgent meaning and, by the 1900s, this idealism and nationalism were taking on disturbing trends:[6] the German League had been founded in 1894 and, four years later, its founder Friedrich Lange gave out his battle cry 'Pure Germanism'. In the educational world too, the wind of change was evident, for voices were being raised against the domination of the 'academic' subjects in the schools (this was, of course, one of the complaints of the newly formed 'Wandervögel'[7]). The nationalistic movements in German society, enthusiastic in their exaltation of the individual and of the irrational elements of the soul, were fully in favour of restricting the academic subjects in schools and were keen that State education should pay more attention to the development of the imagination and of the emotions, so that the individual would be able to rise to his full stature in this new semi-mystic romantic nation.

Kerschensteiner's interpretation of citizenship was a far cry from this open nationalism which was being propagated. Yet, despite the huge differences between them, educationists and others still continued to misinterpret his concept of 'education for citizenship' and Kerschensteiner was left to explain and justify his views as best he could. Finally, ten years after the publication of the prize essay, which had brought 'education for citizenship' to the attention of the educational world, Kerschensteiner was still seeking to expound his views more fully in new books and to justify himself in the eyes of his critics, who still refused to recognize that Kerschensteiner's citizen was essentially a thinking, moral person and not just a subservient State servant:

'The objection which is raised against my demands of the ultimate purpose of education comes from a misunderstanding, which, despite my repeated and detailed statements on the concept of the State and of education for citizenship, fails to recognize that education for citizenship means educating the student to realize the ethical idea of the highest outward Good. He will fulfil this idea through conscious and thoughtful service to the community. My objectors, however, always interpret "education for citizenship" only to mean educating the student to perform blind service to a strictly defined State organism. As soon as they have the honest intention of grasping this basic difference, the misunderstanding will disappear.'[8]

Kerschensteiner's citizen was much more than a tool in the hands of the State. He was a true social being, an active member of a progressing community. The very first community with which man comes into contact, and of which he becomes an integral constituent, is the family community, and it is here that Kerschensteiner would have his citizen form those basic qualities of character necessary for any kind of community life. The child would be subjected in his family life to that interplay of personalities and roles which Kerschensteiner thought to be a mirror of the interdependent forces interweaving in the larger family-community, which was the State-community. In family life he would learn to have consideration for others, selflessness, respect for the ideas and aims of others, honesty and uprightness. He would be taught the role he would play in the progress of the State, and, in the same way that the family fostered the idea of the State-community, the State would foster the idea of the World-community, so that the citizen would be aware of the part which the State played in the progress of the world. He would come to realize that the economic, spiritual, and moral progress of the State would benefit not only the State itself but could also be deployed to help underdeveloped countries in the great humanitarian effort, which is the keynote of all true citizenship:

'Just as the family's task is to foster the State-idea and to prepare its members for State-citizenship, so one could say it is the job of the State to promote the "humanity-idea" of world-citizenship.... If we educate good State-citizens we are also educating good World-citizens.'[9]

EDUCATION AND WORK

How, then, would Kerschensteiner have this ideal citizen educated? One of his most important requirements was that the citizens should acquire the highest degree of trade efficiency of which they were individually capable, for being a citizen entailed being a 'useful' citizen – that is, one who could work to provide his own welfare and contribute to that of his State:

'To be an ideal person, one must first be a useful person. The useful person is the one who acknowledges his own work and that of his countrymen and who possesses the will and the strength to carry it out.'[10]

Or similarly:

'The ultimate aim of all schools which are maintained by public resources is to educate their pupils to become useful citizens. A useful citizen is the one who, through his work, either directly or indirectly, helps so that the aims of the State, a civilized and lawful community, shall be achieved.'[11]

Trade training was to be a basic and fundamental part of Kerschensteiner's educational system, for, according to his philosophy, without efficient workers there could be no efficient citizens:

'Thus the first demand of the individual in the community is that he should be capable and willing to carry out some function in the State; in other words, he should be engaged in some trade, so that he is in a position to further the State's aim, either directly or indirectly. From this, we deduce the school's most basic task. The school must first help each youngster to take up some kind of work in society, to take up some trade and to perform it to the best of his ability. This, of course, is not a task which is concerned with morality, yet it is the basic prerequisite for moral education.

'The school's second task is to accustom the individual to regard his work as a duty which he must fulfil not merely in the interests of his own personal moral and material welfare but also in the interests of the State, which, in turn, makes it possible for each individual to work and support himself, protected by the laws of a civilised community. According to the type of work, it will be easy, difficult or impossible to see in it a direct service to the community. There are many trades where the individual is inspired by this idea of service to the community. There is also a host of other trades which cannot be connected directly with work for the common good. But it will always be possible to make the growing generation conscious, early on in life, that every trade can be regarded as a service which is necessary to the community. We can always make the youngsters aware of the fact that taking up any kind of paid work, however monotonous or modest it may be, brings with it the duty of performing it to the best of one's ability.

'The third and greatest of the school's educational tasks, one which of course demands suitable intellectual and moral gifts in the pupils, is to develop in them the inclination to contribute their part in the furtherance of the State's progress towards the ideal of the moral community. They will do this both through, and apart from, their trade, and not least through working towards the perfection of their own specific moral personality.

'Thus every school, including the elementary school, is given three clearly defined tasks, which, at the same time, embrace the whole purpose of education. They are briefly:

'1. Vocational training, or at least preparation for vocational training.
'2. Making this vocational education a moral education.
'3. Teaching the moral value of the community in which the trade is to be carried out.'[12]

Education and Citizenship · 33

At this point, it must be pointed out that, in German, the word 'Beruf' means not only a 'trade' in the narrow sense in which that word is used in the English language, but also means profession or vocation. It implies the pursuit of any kind of paid work at whatever level, whether physical or intellectual. So, when Kerschensteiner insisted on the value of carrying out a trade, he embraced the fullest possible meaning of that word.

Kerschensteiner, therefore, saw technical trade instruction as being the first stage towards the ultimate goal of education, which was to produce selfless, moral citizens whose greatest desire it was to uphold the moral pillars of the State and of their fellow men. Another subject of study which Kerschensteiner regarded as being imperative for the citizen in the constitutional, democratic State was regular instruction in the composition of the State and the concept of the State-ideal. Up till that time, the German population had had little opportunity to learn of the social, economic, and spiritual forces which all combine to form a State; the male population had been granted the vote in 1871 yet few of them really knew much of the role and function of the State, of its duties to the people who constituted it, and of their duties to that same State which made civilized existence possible for them. Kerschensteiner saw that it was of vital importance for the schools to give instruction in civics, so that their pupils would become aware of the diverging, yet unifying, forces which all combined to form the pulsating organism of the State. For an enthusiasm to do one's best for the advancement of the State could only be born from a complete and thorough knowledge and understanding of the State itself, and from a deep sympathy with its ethical aims and ideals.

THE PRIZE ESSAY

It was in his prize essay that Kerschensteiner first committed to paper these thoughts which were to be of revolutionary significance in the German educational scheme, and, since they immediately evoked a lively reaction in educational circles, they deserve being quoted here at considerable length. On the question of how the modern constitutional State should fulfil its functions (which Kerschensteiner defined as being to further its own preservation and the welfare of its members) Kerschensteiner wrote:

'If the modern State recognizes the citizenship of all its members, if it gives them the right and duty of assisting the State to fulfil its functions in the interests of the community, if, under certain conditions, the individual can be awarded what may be a decisive voice in national affairs, both in the field of civil law and international politics – then the answer to our question is near at hand. It is simply this: the State fulfils its functions by giving everyone as extensive an education as possible, one which educates its pupils to have:

'(a) a knowledge of the functions of the State, and
'(b) the highest degree of personal efficiency.

'In other words, the modern State achieves its aim quickest by giving each of its members an education which gives him a general understanding of the functions of a State; it is an education which makes him able and willing to fill his place in the State organism as well as he possibly can.'[13]

Concerning civic education Kerschensteiner wrote:

'Here there is no question of giving a general education with its theoretical inquiry into the functions of the State, on which a system of social ethics or a general theory of government could be based. For several reasons this side of civic education must be limited to the more modest aim of pointing out, in a clear and effective way, the dependence of the pupil's particular financial and social interests of his work on the interests of his fellow citizens and of his native country. These reasons include the intellectual immaturity of the pupils in question, the short time available for an extensive intellectual training under existing conditions, the less certain influence on the will which is effected by instruction alone, and the absolute necessity of providing for all-round professional efficiency, without which civic usefulness would be greatly impaired.

'We must exclude from our teaching every theory which goes beyond the intellectual maturity of the pupils. . . .

'As a means of ensuring that personal efficiency which enables the pupil to take up the place in society awarded him by his ability, training for trade efficiency must be given pride of place. Training in professional efficiency is the "conditio sine qua non" of all civic education. At the same time as this aim is being pursued and the youngsters are being educated to be joyful and efficient in their work,

Education and Citizenship · 35

those very civic virtues are being developed which must be regarded as the basis of all higher moral training: conscientiousness, industry, perseverance, self restraint, and devotion to a strenuous life.

'By showing the interdependence of individual interests it may be possible to develop the highest of civic virtues – self-control, justice, and devotion to the interests of the community. How far education will be successful in this respect depends, of course, on how much our educational arrangements allow the pupil to be *actively* involved with his environment and to what an extent they allow him to apply the sympathetic interests which we have awoken in him. For virtues can only be formed through action; Aristotle[14] has taught us this much. This is also true of the second aim which education for personal efficiency embraces, which is training in a sensible, hygienic way of life, so that the pupil is fit for military service. Here, too, we shall have to see to it that the pupil not only acquires the necessary insight but that the opportunity for using it is also given to him whenever possible.

'To sum up, the first aim of education for those leaving the elementary school is training for trade efficiency and love of work. With these is connected the training of those elementary virtues which efficiency and love of work have in their train – conscientiousness, industry, perseverance, responsibility, self-restraint, and devotion to an active life.

'Following close on that, the second aim must be pursued, which is, to gain an insight into the relation of individuals to one another and to the State and to understand the laws of health. This knowledge and insight must then be used actively in the exercise of self-control, justice, devotion to duty, and in leading a sensible life characterized by a strong feeling of personal responsibility.

'One can call the first aim that of technical education, the second, that of moral and intellectual education. But one must be conscious of the fact that the first aim also has high moments of intellectual and moral education, and that the second aim can only be attained through the first and as a continuation of it.'[15]

Thus the two main precepts on which Kerschensteiner's philosophy of education rest are that successful training for citizenship entails training the pupil in trade efficiency, and, simultaneously, educating him to be a person imbued with moral principles of the highest order –

so that when the opportunity presents itself, he will willingly and joyfully use those skills and qualities of character which he has acquired in his training for trade efficiency in the pursuit of those moral principles which he recognizes to be of the utmost importance for the continued advancement of the State.

As to the age groups for which this education for citizenship would be at its most fruitful, Kerschensteiner rejected the elementary school pupils as being unsuitable. He had already written of the limitations of the elementary schools in his report and new curricula which had been published in 1899:

'One must be conscious of the fact that the best that can be achieved in the elementary school – apart from the discipline which it is its duty to give – consists in giving few or lasting stimuli. It is not remotely capable of unfolding those buds from which the character will be bound to develop later.'[16]

In the same way that Rousseau would postpone preoccupation with certain subjects, such as history or religion, until the pupil had reached an age when he had gained a certain mental, emotional, and spiritual maturity and had enjoyed a certain amount of experience of life itself, so Kerschensteiner felt that education for citizenship would be more effectively carried out among the older, continuation school pupils, who were already standing on the path to citizenship by the mere fact that they had taken up employment and were thus helping to provide for their own keep. It was with pupils in the continuation schools that teaching in trade efficiency would be the most successful, since trade instruction was of great relevance to them in their new role of 'worker'. At the same time, the instruction in civics would be grasped more readily by these maturer pupils who were beginning to be aware of the role which they and their work played in society.

This period of apprenticeship, which, in Germany, lasted until the youngster attained the age of seventeen or eighteen, was to form the first of Kerschensteiner's three stages of citizenship education; the second stage was to be carried out during the period when the youngster was a journeyman (a period of at least five years) and the third and concluding stage was to take place during military service. (Since the authority of the State assumed such a great importance in Kerschensteiner's theories, Kerschensteiner would be unlikely to understand the viewpoint of those who reject military service as being contrary

KERSCHENSTEINER'S THEORIES AND THE CONTINUATION SCHOOLS

to Christian principles.) However, it was with the first two of these stages that Kerschensteiner was mainly concerned, and it is with those same two stages that the remainder of this book will deal.

It was to the continuation schools that Kerschensteiner attached the most significant role in education for citizenship, for these schools were to form the basic skills and qualities which would be the foundation necessary for the next two stages. Since their teaching was of vital importance for the training of real 'men' and 'citizens', Kerschensteiner insisted that continuation school attendance should be compulsory for *all* youngsters who had left the ordinary elementary school. As has already been shown, despite regulations which dealt with compulsory attendance of the general continuation schools, there were still many German youngsters who did not have the opportunity of attending such schools. Even those who were attending them often reaped little benefit, since instruction was given in evening classes when the pupils were liable to be very tired after their day's work. Kerschensteiner therefore stressed that it was equally imperative for the classes at continuation school to be given not in the evening but during the daytime, when the pupils' minds and bodies would be fresh and active, thus enabling the instruction to fall on more fertile ground.

Efforts to get away from the form of the general continuation school were already being made by various other individual educators in different parts of the country who realized the ineffectiveness of the existing system. In the 1880s Friedrich Rücklin had introduced a new system of continued education in Baden, whereby the teaching was centred on the various trades and on business administration. Specialist teachers were brought in from the different trades to give instruction in these new schools, at which attendance was compulsory for six hours a week. In Leipzig, too, the continuation school teaching was under constant revision by the well-known educationist Oskar Pache. In his continuation schools trade teaching was made the basis of the curriculum in all classes whose pupils were employed in the same trade. Where a class consisted of pupils from a variety of trades the teaching was centred on a study of the local area where the pupils lived (die schöne Heimat).[17] However, it must be pointed out that although technical training was available both in Rücklin's and Pache's schools, this training was not practical training such as Kerschensteiner had in mind, but consisted basically of a theoretical training in the fields of management, commerce, and administration.

However successful these restricted innovations by Rücklin and Pache were, they were overshadowed by Kerschensteiner's dramatic proposals for the reorganization of the Munich continuation school system. Although the problem of general *versus* professional education had arisen before, it was Kerschensteiner who brought it right to the forefront of educational discussions after the publication of his prize essay, in which his ideas had been put forward so forcibly. Trade education *versus* general education was a subject which came to the centre of educational controversy, and even in the last third of the twentieth century it still bears great significance.

Despite the obvious differences in the organization of Kerschensteiner's curriculum and the traditional Herbartian curriculum, Kerschensteiner nevertheless had several features in common with Herbart, whose educational philosophy and that of his followers had held sway through the whole of the nineteenth century. They were both in complete agreement that the ultimate aim of all education was a *moral* one, i.e. the education of the pupil to be a man of character, inspired by the ideals of honesty, tolerance, moral courage, and selfless dedication to the forces of the Good. For both educators, training of character, and, in Platonic language, turning the eye to the Good, were the aims of all education. Only their methods of achieving these ends were different: Herbart maintained that the curriculum should be on a wide basis, covering a number of 'general' subjects, which presented opportunities for moral education. Some subjects in the Herbartian system lent themselves more easily than others to moral education: for instance, in the teaching of history or literature special stress would be laid on certain persons or peoples who presented some desirable trait of character such as courage, perseverance in the face of hardship, kindness to the weak, self-sacrifice, etc. For Herbart at the beginning of the nineteenth century, professional training, such as Kerschensteiner envisaged, possessed no *educational* value whatsoever.

In the Kerschensteiner system, however, it was precisely by means of the vocational training that the essential qualities of character were to be formed. For here the mind would be at its most receptive, since professional training bore very great relevance to the daily life and livelihood of the pupils, who would be eager to further their education along these lines. During this period of professional training the schools were so to habituate their pupils to observe certain codes of behaviour and standards of work, that when the age of insight and maturity came they would recognize these principles as being of true value and would continue to uphold them. The lessons in civics, which would form an integral part of the curriculum in the continuation schools, were intended to show the pupil how these moral precepts and qualities of character, which had been formed in him, could best be used in the service of mankind.

Professional training was not an end in itself, but only the means to an end, for:

'Vocational training leads to character training.'[18]

4 · Character Training

INTEREST

Kerschensteiner's many years of teaching experience had brought him into a very close and sincere contact with pupils from all walks of life and of all ages and interests. His continued experience of children, both at work and at play, had furnished him with understanding of child development and psychology – of the way a child thinks and acts, feels and believes, plays and works. As to the child's mental activity and receptivity, numerous examples had shown him that the child's mental activity did not remain constant but fluctuated according to the intensity of *interest* which the child directed on to the task in hand. This principle, which had impressed itself upon him time and time again in the fields outside Schweinfurt and in the drab Nürnberg classrooms, was strengthened and proved over and over again during his investigations into the existing general continuation schools.

There were, of course, several external factors which could help to explain the inertia prevalent in these schools, but to Kerschensteiner it was obvious that even if building space, allotment of hours, and the curriculum subjects had all conformed to an ideal pattern, the teaching in the general continuation schools was still doomed to failure; the real cause lay not in the general conditions but was due to a basic deficiency in the spirit of the schools. There was no *soul* in either the teaching or the learning, for there was an utter lack of interest in the subjects studied and, consequently, a complete lack of inner excitement and activity in the pupils. How much more mentally receptive and actively involved would be children who were attracted to their school subjects by a deep interest. How much more eagerly would they approach the subject and follow up every line of investigation, taxing their own ability with determination when examining, verifying, and deducing new data, courageously persevering in the face of difficulties and disappointments. Surely the subjects to be taught in the continuation schools should rather be those which appealed to the child, subjects in which he showed some degree of interest and ability. Only in this case would the pupil devote the maximum amount of concentration and effort to his studies. If his work were of interest to him he would take pride in it and would exert himself to perform it *well*, spurred on by that inner urge and excitement of spirit which beget works of quality and creativity.

Kerschensteiner saw the many different kinds of interest as being the pivot on which all education should turn. Basically, all human interests resulted from needs:

'The ultimate roots of interests are always bodily, spiritual or mental needs.'[1]

There were certain basic, instinctive needs and urges common to all mankind, which must be satisfied: the need for food and drink, the need for a certain material and economic security, home and employment; the instincts of love and hate, self-assertion and mental activity, the desire for mental or physical achievement. Apart from these basic interests which constituted part of man's physical, mental, and spiritual make-up, Kerschensteiner conceived of another group of interests, which he termed functional interests, which could and should play an important part in the review of the organization of the school curriculum.

A functional interest was an interest which was purely of a utilitarian nature, i.e. where there was no interest in the object or the task for its own sake, but where an interest had to be aroused for it, because the object or task in hand was necessary for the achievement of the ultimate end, on which the true interest was centred. To make this clearer Kerschensteiner quoted the example of the child who had been told of the works of a foreign author, about whom the child then became most enthusiastic. The author's works had not been translated from the foreign language, and so the only way for the child to make the acquaintanceship of the author would be for him to learn that foreign language. (Children who respond in such a way must be rare, but Kerschensteiner put forward the argument.) In this case, the interest in the language was purely functional, for the language provided no interest in itself and was simply a means to an end. The example served to illustrate Kerschensteiner's theory that, even if the pupil showed no enthusiasm or interest in his learning for its own sake, at least a functional interest could be developed if he were shown that his work and learning were not being carried out purely for their own sake but that they all served some further purpose or aim. Kerschensteiner's theories also admitted the possibility of transfer of interest, for it was quite feasible for a functional interest to develop, in time, into an interest in the task of work *per se*.

Kerschensteiner's preoccupation with theories of interest and his conclusion that teaching could only be successful when the pupils' interest in the subject matter was cultivated, was a principle which had made little headway in German education, for up till that time German schools had concerned themselves much more with the knowledge which the child was to be taught than with a study of the child himself. By thus directing the attention of German educationists to child study Kerschensteiner was to make a lasting contribution to education, for his theories were to mark the commencement, in Germany, of the movement towards psychology in the education of the adolescent.

Applying his views on the function of interest to the general continuation schools, Kerschensteiner saw that the teaching in those schools would achieve some measure of success only when it removed from the curriculum those wholly academic subjects, to which such a large proportion of teaching time was devoted, for which the vast majority of their pupils were unsuited. Instead, the schools should heed the true interests of the average fourteen-year-old, which were purely egocentric ones. The average adolescent worker was not interested in academics but in *himself* and in his newly formed way of life; he was fascinated by his new status of 'worker' and by his own self-importance. His overruling desire was to become an efficient worker at his trade. Thus Kerschensteiner maintained that it was imperative that the general continuation schools should be changed into trade schools, where the whole of the curriculum would be centred on a study of the trade in which the pupils were employed.

ALTRUISM

In an investigation into the causes which initiated man's actions, Kerschensteiner concluded in his prize essay that 'the actions of mankind are, in the main, determined by two influences. Hunger and love; egoism and altruism – these form the motives of the world.'[2]

Egoism he interpreted not in its narrow context of being merely man's pursuit of his own personal selfish desires and interests to further his own material ends but saw it as being basically the expression of man's innate impulse towards self-preservation and the search for personal happiness. It also represented the individual's efforts to achieve the aims and ambitions which he had set himself, whether those ambitions be directed to his own ends or for the benefit of others. Even in apparently benevolent and humanitarian acts the roots of the deed could sometimes be seen to lie not in altruism, as the doer himself might suppose, but in egoism:

'We are often deceived as to the real motives of our deliberate, non-spontaneous decisions. Often we think that we are acting quite disinterestedly and that we are spurred on by a love for something outside us. We think that we have an overpowering sense of duty which urges us to act in the service of our neighbour. But, if we really make a careful examination of our hearts we see that the decisive factor is really the ego, even if it is only the expression of the unconscious instinct to remain true to our better self. And so, if we really search, we can occasionally find the dregs of egoism in acts of deepest sympathy, purest love and sincerest benevolence.'[3]

Character Training · 43

While both egoism and altruism were factors inherent in the nature of man, it was the strength of the altruistic motives which formed the essential characteristic of Kerschensteiner's citizens, who always showed themselves ready to devote themselves willingly and with selfless dedication to the interests and welfare of their fellow men. If the altruistic motives were to overcome the egoistic motives, educational and environmental factors would have to play a great part in effecting the change. Thus Kerschensteiner conceived of one of the basic tasks of all schools as being to seize every opportunity which presented itself to mould, develop, and perfect the innate factor of altruism, the seeds of which were to be found in every child.

But how was this power of altruism to be singled out and nurtured in the child? One cannot order a child to be altruistic. Kerschensteiner pointed out that no amount of lecturing or sermonizing would or ever could produce in the child that inner feeling and will for altruism, which are to be found at the source of all altruistic deeds. It had been accepted since the time of Aristotle that only deeds could form virtues, in other words, that virtue could never be acquired through passive receptivity but only through action. Or, as Goethe had said, a talent is formed in quiet, but character is formed in the crowds of the world.

Thus, it was of primary importance that the schools should give their pupils the opportunities to undertake altruistic deeds. Of equal importance was Kerschensteiner's demand that the pupils should be given an insight into and an understanding of their fellow-beings, for altruistic deeds could only be born from bonds of sympathy which the pupils felt towards their fellows. It was therefore up to the school to foster the formation of these bonds of sympathy which could reach out between men.

Kerschensteiner advocated also that it was not only the altruistic forces which should be nurtured in the pupils but that even the egoistic impulses should be deployed in the service of altruism. The schools should skilfully direct the egoistical pursuits into channels of a more altruistic nature until finally, with the development of a mature and ripened intellect, the pupils themselves would wilfully and willingly take up the cause of altruism, inspired by their conviction of its intrinsic value and worth:

'While it (egoism) always remains the stronger instinct in animals, it becomes subdued in man under the influence of a suitable education, in which discipline and habit form the basis on which is built the influence of a later developing maturity. A progressing insight into the bonds which link the welfare of the individual and that of the State (such as is manifested in an understanding of the dependence of the individual's well-being on the well-being of his family, his work associates, the members of his local community and of the State) brings an even greater influence to bear on our moral judgements and enables us to accept more and more readily the fact that the most valuable motives for our action are those which have universal validity. While in this way the selfish force of the lower egoistic instincts, which are directed towards our personal welfare, becomes weaker, at the same time the sympathetic impulses unfold and perfect themselves. This development and refinement of the sympathetic impulses takes place in proportion as an *active* life among our family, workmates, fellow citizens, and so on causes our conceptions of our thinking and sentient fellow-beings to increase in depth and breadth.'[4]

Kerschensteiner had no doubts as to the stage in the pupil's education at which this education for altruism, or, in its broader aspect, education for citizenship, would be the most successful. It would be at its most efficient and successful at the stage in the pupil's school career when self-interest and egoism were at their strongest, for these could then be diverted into altruistic paths. The most fruitful period was therefore that of the apprenticeship years, characterized as they were by the egoistic interests of personal efficiency and professional advancement. Here, in vocational training, would the seeds of altruism yield their richest fruit:

'How then shall we tackle the question of educating the young citizen to develop an altruism which is born of insight? There only seems one answer possible to this question – at his work . . . The vast majority of young people are engaged in some kind of employment and want to advance by means of their work. Their interests are centred on their job and nearly all the youngsters are to be won over through this sphere of interest. If we win the boy over in this way, we also gain his confidence and with that we can guide him both intellectually and morally.'[5]

Thus, in order to educate its pupils to become altruistic beings ready to devote their powers and skills to the service of mankind, Kerschensteiner's school had two tasks: firstly, to develop the character

Character Training · 45

of the pupils; and secondly, to give them a knowledge of the altruistic purposes which would inspire them to use their intellect, skills, and qualities of character in the interests of their fellow men. Both of these tasks were to be achieved by using professional education as the training ground, since this was where the young person's true interests lay.

THE CONCEPT OF CHARACTER

The question of character, and the means by which it could be developed, was a subject which afforded Kerschensteiner a great deal of interest, for the principle that not the acquisition of knowledge but the training of character should be the aim of all education, was one which had filled his thoughts and actions for many years before he had entered administration. In 1912 he published the book *Character and Character Training*,[6] which dealt with the subject extensively.

The interpretations of the concept of character have been many and varied, but Kerschensteiner's own interpretation was that the basic ingredients of the intelligible character were four in number, and, although one of them would be likely to dominate, all four would nevertheless blend together to form a balanced, harmonious unity. The four factors were: will, clarity of judgement, sensibility, and the ability to become innerly 'involved' in a situation.

The most important of these, in Kerschensteiner's view, was the first, will. It was a quality to which the schools should pay very great attention in their work concerning the training of character. Kerschensteiner conceived of the will as being of two kinds: there was firstly the will-power which brought forth qualities of a more passive nature, qualities such as a noble patience, tolerance, and perseverance. The second kind of will was of the kind which evoked qualities of a more active nature. This type of will was also most important and bore a direct relationship to the advancement of society, for of this kind of will were born action and deeds, the very pillars of civilization, since civilization was created and upheld by action and deeds, and not by thought alone.

The second quality of character, clarity of judgement, or the ability to think clearly and logically, was a quality vital to every person living in Kerschensteiner's ideal democratic State who would thus be required to participate in the political and social activity of that State.

46 · *Georg Kerschensteiner*

The citizen must be able to think clearly and concisely: his thinking must not be dulled or influenced by personal, subjective factors, but must at all times be objective, thorough, and conscientious. Having correctly observed and assessed the matter in question, he must be capable of drawing some kind of conclusion and of verifying that conclusion or deduction by logical and systematic methods. He must be able to pass judgement and to make a clear and well-defined decision. Kerschensteiner saw that the schools had a significant role to play in giving their pupils the opportunity to use those gifts of intellect with which they were endowed. The pupils should be encouraged to take pleasure in thinking, whether it be thinking towards a set purpose or thinking for its own sake.

The third quality, sensibility, Kerschensteiner defined as being 'the readiness of the soul to be moved, and its ability to be moved in a variety of ways'.[7] This was a quality to be found especially strong in the artist. Among the remainder of the population also it could be manifested in various ways: it could find expression as tact, as an instinctive consideration for the feelings of others, as presence of mind, as the quick and instinctive appraisal of a situation and the ability to adapt oneself to it. Kerschensteiner thought that this quality could be trained, to a certain extent, if the child's observation were cultivated and the various situations in life which inspired this feeling were brought to his attention. Sensibility was a quality which was evoked essentially through contact with fellow men, and so, by seeing to it that their pupils were brought into early contact with people and different situations and experiences in life, the schools could contribute their share in the development of this quality.

The final basic quality of character was the ability to involve one's whole being in the accomplishment of the task in hand. Kerschensteiner understood this quality, for instance, as being the quality which distinguished the real artist, actor, or musician from the virtuoso. The true artist put the entire concentration of his whole mind and soul on the work to be performed: his soul became so involved, that the artist's whole being became identified with the work, so that he was completely unaware of any external factors. Kerschensteiner's definition of this quality was: 'The degree to which the soul is gripped by perceptions or ideas, and the extent and duration of that state of soul' – or, in other words – 'It means the extent, depth, and durability of the waves of emotion, which accompany the perceptions, ideas, and concepts coming and going in the stream of consciousness.'[8] This ability of the soul to be gripped by some idea or ideal Kerschensteiner saw as being brought into play, particularly, when man came into contact with the concepts and ideas which bore relevance to man and his destiny; in short, with the moral concepts, of whose true value every citizen was convinced and in whose service he would find his own self-fulfilment.

These, then, were the four basic factors in Kerschensteiner's concept of character, which all fused together to form a harmonious unity. Concerning the influence which the schools could bring to bear in the successful training of character, Kerschensteiner made it quite clear that, while the schools would undoubtedly have a beneficial effect, it was not within their powers completely to change the character of a child; they could only develop and promote the qualities of character which the child already possessed. The schools could never *give* character, they could only *develop* it and see that it was used to the proper ends. Character was like a river, in that we could not increase its *strength*, but what we could do was to give it a change of direction and a certain goal.

THE 'ACTIVITY SCHOOL'[9]

But how can the character be trained? Kerschensteiner's answer to this question was the following: 'Character is not to be gained by reading books or listening to sermons but by continuous and steadily applied work.'[10] This precept, namely, that the development of character can only be effected through serious and conscientious activity, through work, whatever type of work it may be, is a precept which forms the leitmotif behind Kerschensteiner's organisation of a new type of school which would pulsate with activity and work, and where the objects of that work and activity corresponded so much to the interests of the pupil that he would not regard them as a duty to be performed, but as a pleasurable occupation.

'It is usually irrelevant what form educative work should take. There appears to be only one necessary condition, namely, that the worker can perform it cheerfully. This is mostly the case when the pupil is interested in his work. It is unimportant *where* work disciplines a man, whether at the study desk or at the easel, at the bench or at the loom, out in the fields or in the workshop, working in manufacture or in the service of practical charity. For there is one thing common to all upright, serious work, namely, that it exercises the powers of will, on which are based the most important civic virtues – diligence, care, conscientiousness, perseverance, attention, honesty, patience, self-control, and devotion to a firm disinterested aim. Of course, these virtues must, later on, be fostered by insight into the necessity of leading a moral life, but this insight can only be effective when the germs which it has to bring to perfection are already developed.'[11]

Kerschensteiner's new 'activity' elementary schools were to be establishments which provided amply for development of character. and which, to this end, would use every method to ensure that activity was the keynote of all school work. The pupil was no longer to have knowledge and facts pushed into him by books and recitative learning. Instead, the knowledge would be presented to him in such a way that full demands were made on his own mental resources: he would need to be observant, to analyse and compare, to call on his own experiences, to *think*. The existing school was to be transformed into a school whose teaching so inspired and interested the pupil that he would take pleasure in taxing his own mental and physical abilities, and in setting himself even more difficult tasks, encouraged by his past achievements and successes. It was to be a school which adapted its teaching to suit the needs of the pupil – in contrast to the existing schools, which forced too much academic knowledge into minds which were not yet ripe enough to assimilate it. Pestalozzi's precept that the child, as a product of his environment, should be educated to be a part of that environment and should therefore be given the necessary skills and knowledge, was one of the fundamental motives of the school. Every provision and facility was to be made available for the manifold development of the pupil and especial attention was to be paid to the unfolding of his innate gifts and talents, whether they be of an intellectual, social, or manual nature.

THE EDUCATIVE VALUE OF PRACTICAL WORK

This new school which Kerschensteiner had in mind was to stress many more aspects of the child's development than did any other type of existing school, for all the other teaching establishments only tried to accomplish, on a smaller scale, what the well-established Gymnasien were doing, i.e. they aimed solely at developing the child's intellect. This they hoped to achieve by means of the study of purely academic courses. Kerschensteiner, however, was convinced that the child's successful development could be furthered in ways other than by a study of the traditional 'academic' subjects: one such way was by conscientious work at the handicrafts. In all aspects of handwork, whatever the material used, the pupil would learn those basic qualities which it was the school's aim to further – diligence and industry, carefulness and attention to detail, cleanliness and honesty, the determination to succeed.

First of all, however, it must be firmly established what Kerschensteiner really understood by 'handwork'. By 'handwork' he meant not the mechanical pursuit of manual work but, instead, productive manual work which was very closely accompanied by mental effort. For only when the two were closely combined would this practical work possess any truly *educative* value. Handiwork, crafts, practical work, call it what we will, stood very high in Kerschensteiner's estimation for its value in helping to develop the virtues and qualities which the pupil would require throughout life: yet it received very little attention from his contemporary German educationists, who, instead, concentrated purely on the academic subjects. In this sphere, too, Kerschensteiner was to set a new trend.

Despite the scorn with which some educationists treated practical work, Kerschensteiner saw it as a response to one of man's basic impulses, an impulse on which the whole of civilization found its roots, since it was from practical handwork that mental work developed. It was craftsmanship which had produced all those monuments of past civilization such as cathedrals and works of art, which bore testimony to man's creative urge. It was a precondition for the advancement of society. Even in Kerschensteiner's times, the State still required many more manual workers than brain workers, and it was for this reason, too, that the schools, in their capacity as establishments for vocational preparation, should provide ample opportunity for the pupils' needs for practical work to be satisfied.

In Kerschensteiner's estimation, 90 per cent of all the children at the elementary school had thoroughly practical interests and derived a great deal of enjoyment from all types of practical work, especially creative practical work. This interest was often accompanied by an aptitude for handicrafts, and the child's enthusiasm grew in proportion as he could see the concrete results of his innate urge to create. Yet this enormous field of human activity, for which the child had a deep and enthusiastic interest – and where he could therefore best be reached by educative influences – remained completely unexplored in the German schools. Kerschensteiner was determined to have this fruitful field of educative work introduced into those schools which would gain most benefit from it – the elementary school and the continuation school. In both of these schools the pupil was happiest when engaged on some kind of practical work, and would therefore be at his most productive and efficient in this type of work. Manual work corresponded to his innate desire for activity, and at the same time it gave him the opportunity for creativity: it was an interest completely *natural* to him.

Here was a sphere of activity which was admirably suitable as a basis for character training, for the child's spontaneous interest and liking for practical work would spur him on to hard, conscientious work, which was the training ground for all civic virtues. The task of the teacher would be made easier too, for, since the child's interest was there by nature, the teacher would no longer be required to think up ingenious, and not always successful, methods for arousing it artificially, as he did when teaching academic subjects, which bore little relevance to the child's immediate life and environment. The pupils' natural attraction towards handicrafts and manual work invariably led to pleasure in this type of work – a most important feature in all successful education. That people should *enjoy* their work, and more important still, that they should enjoy work which they undertook in the interests of others, was the aim of all education:

'Education of the people means leading them systematically to take a common pleasure in work.'[12]

Kerschensteiner was determined that his contemporaries should recognize the validity of handiwork as a subject in its own right, and was eager that it should be introduced as a compulsory subject in the elementary school. In the continuation school, moreover, the scope of practical work far surpassed that which it had in the elementary school, for not only did the pupils' *natural* interests and aptitudes focus thereon but, since the majority of the young people were to be engaged in manual trades, there was also an external pressure which turned their attention to practical work, for their material and economic welfare depended to a large extent on their trade efficiency. The continuation school pupil would never be more mentally receptive than he was at the workshop bench. In the continuation school, therefore, practical instruction was not merely to be inserted organically into the curriculum as an extra subject but was to be made the very foundation for the acquisition of all theoretical knowledge and was to be given pride of place at the *centre* of the curriculum.

Here at the workshop bench those qualities of character were to be developed which the pupil would need in his later life. His will-power, the most important of Kerschensteiner's factors in character, was to be strengthened, for the will and determination to succeed and the perseverance and never-flagging spirit were qualities needed in the pursuit of all manual skills. The youngster would learn to think clearly, for the precision in practical work and in the mathematical calculations it required could only be carried out by logical, systematic and conscientious thinking. He would be trained to form habits of honesty and cleanliness, punctuality and tidiness; he would be taught to appreciate the value of doing a job *well*, however humble or insignificant the job may appear to be. To teach the boy to take pride in his work was one of the most important tasks of all schools, for their pupils should never be permitted to be satisfied with work which was only of mediocre quality, but should be content only with giving of their very best. All work should be finished off, and should have as much concentration directed to its satisfactory completion as it had in its commencement: it was vital for the workers in the State to take pride in their work – not only to enjoy performing it but also to obtain personal *satisfaction* from it. Whatever the work, whether it was highly specialized, academic, or of a humble nature, it would be of no use to the community if it were not completed *well*. It must again be emphasized that Kerschensteiner insisted that this practical work must not finally take the form of mechanical, repetitive exercises. A certain amount of mechanical work must of course be completed first, in order to provide the pupils with the basic skills necessary for the pursuit of the work. The final work, however, should be of such a nature that the pupils' minds were greatly taxed. They should be encouraged to think and compare, so that they arrived at the true road to education – where they were not *taught*, but where they taught themselves and where they *discovered* through their own experience. Intensive, independent intellectual work at clearly defined tasks was the only way to true education – and practical work provided the basis:

'True education is always attained through work: it only acquires its strength from serious, intensive, practical, productive activity. The craftsman, the farmer, the artist, the scholar all reach true human greatness through independent work at definite tasks.'[13]

By basing the curriculum of the continuation schools on education for trade efficiency Kerschensteiner thus achieved the first of his aims, namely, to 'further trade efficiency and, with that, the pupil's joy in his work'. How this egoism was to be converted to altruism will be shown in the following chapter.

5 · The Organization of the Schools

A BROAD BASIS FOR TRADE INSTRUCTION

As a result of his inspiring work in Munich, Kerschensteiner's name was soon being mentioned in educational discussions, not only in Germany but throughout Europe. If Kerschensteiner's plans were adopted, the pattern of the existing system would be changed considerably, for in addition to the raising of the school-leaving age, which he had effected, the whole nature of the continuation school curriculum would be altered. No longer were the traditional 'general' subjects to dominate the curriculum. In their place was to be substituted a sound course of trade instruction, which would be used as a basis for education for citizenship. His aim was summed up again as follows:

'Everyone knows from his own experience that a subject becomes interesting as soon as it shows some relevance to what usually occupies one's thoughts. And so the whole art of teaching must aim at connecting up citizenship, in as unobtrusive a way as possible, with the subjects in which the pupil is by nature most interested. . . . The industrious continuation school pupil is spurred on by an interest in extensive and sound practical work and not by a desire for bookish wisdom or fancy precepts. . . . (The workshops) correspond best to the pupil's egoistic nature. . . . However, they are not the aim itself but only the means by which our educational aim is to be achieved. We achieve this aim by connecting what we really want to teach the pupil with the instruction in practical work: the more numerous and skilful the connexions, the more we shall achieve our aim.'[1]

All the other knowledge which Kerschensteiner thought necessary for the young apprentice, knowledge pertaining to his particular trade, was to be connected as much as possible with his experiences in the school workshop. It was not to be superimposed artificially on to his practical work, but it was important that it should have the practical work as its very basis. The extent to which the subjects allowed themselves to be related to the workshop instruction depended on the scope of the particular subjects involved: some subjects, of course, lent themselves to this more easily than others. Arithmetic, for instance, was a very suitable subject in this respect, since it could easily find relevance to the work undertaken in the workshop. The practical work could be consolidated, too, by the pupil drawing plans of the various stages in the work and making models. Such plans as these for the incorporation into the curriculum of subjects which could be put to practical use by the pupils form today's norm in schools of all kinds, but Kerschensteiner's pedagogical significance for education at the close of the last century cannot be underestimated. His ideas for revitalizing the contemporary German education system were a pointer to the flags of the educational reform movements, hoisted in the 1920s in Germany.

Kerschensteiner pointed out that other subjects, too, would be needed by the young student if he was to become an efficient worker, the precondition of true citizenship. He must not only be taught the skills of his trade but also the tools of his trade. He must be able to recognize the different tools or machines in use in the school workshop of his trade and must be familiar with their purpose and usage. He must also have a knowledge of the elementary laws of hygiene and first aid. Another subject whose teaching could be centred on the school workshop was bookkeeping, for its various aspects, such as running costs, buying and selling costs, questions regarding payment and banking, etc., could all be treated with reference to the workshop itself.

Kerschensteiner also believed that the apprentice should no longer be choked within the narrow confines of his own particular branch of the trade but should have his outlook broadened through a knowledge of the functions and value of the whole of the trade or industry in which he was employed. He should be given instruction in the various raw materials used in his trade, and should know from what part of the world they came and the main geographical conditions of the areas concerned; he should be made familiar with the methods and processes by which they were converted into the marketable product, and should be aware of the position and importance of his own particular work to the trade as a whole. He should also be introduced to the literary works of leading men in his industry or of leading personalities in the labour or social movement, where he could see language deployed in the service of the community. Also, in addition to a sound knowledge of the tools, methods, and materials needed by his industry, Kerschensteiner advocated that the worker should be given instruction on the legal aspects connected with his work.

Some of Kerschensteiner's precepts may well seem outdated to modern schools of thought, but his work on aspects such as these is still revolutionary in the English industrial pattern, where the youngster leaves school and enters a trade or industry without having undergone compulsory periods of training and instruction. In England, where there is no compulsory industrial training, the number of industrial accidents in 1964 rose to 268,648, showing an increase of 31 per cent on the figures for the preceding year. Doubtless many of these could have been avoided if the employees were obliged to undergo compulsory, planned factory training, which would treat safety at work as one of its subjects. Kerschensteiner was determined to ensure also that the German youth knew enough not only about his work but also about labour relations, about the rights both of the employer and the employee, about the various social benefits which were available, about the work of the different trade societies and chambers of trade. Being a worker was not enough. He must be an *efficient* worker in full command of *all* the skills and knowledge necessary for efficiency.

These trade subjects taught in the continuation schools would, of course, be varied to suit the needs of the different trades in which the pupils were employed: typing would be given to girls engaged in commerce, foreign languages to waiters and shopkeepers – to quote just two examples. Whatever the trade of the pupil, the same principle would be followed, namely, that the first step to citizenship lay in trade efficiency and that it was the task of the schools to produce good and happy workers.

ALTRUISM AND CIVICS

Yet, while this trade efficiency was to be the foundation of good citizenship, trade training was only the first stage in the process of forming citizens. It was the egoistic stage and had yet to cede to the strength of altruism, for the second stage in the education of Kerschensteiner's citizens was 'To accustom the pupil to put his trade efficiency and joy in work to the service of fellow pupils and fellow citizens.'[2]

It has already been shown that Kerschensteiner considered that altruism developed in proportion as the pupils became truly aware of their fellow men and of the forces uniting all men. One could not become truly altruistic until one's sensibility towards one's fellow men and one's consciousness of them as sentient beings had developed, for only out of an awareness of their feelings and of the situation in which they were placed could any sympathetic impulses arise in the observer. Thus, in this second stage of education for citizenship the characteristic of sensibility – 'the readiness of the soul to be moved, and its ability to be moved in a variety of ways' – was the factor to be developed especially, while at the same time, by educating for trade efficiency, the schools developed clarity of thinking and strengthened the will-power. This characteristic of sensibility, essentially one of the emotions, could be evoked through a close and constant contact with one's fellow citizens, from which an understanding with them would be created. The offspring of this true understanding was a true sympathy, whereby one's soul became so great as to be moved by the experience of another person to the same extent as it would be moved by a personal experience:

'True pity can only be experienced by the man who can put himself in the position of the person to be pitied. The deepest pity is felt by the one who has himself suffered the same or a similar sorrow, of which he retains a vivid recollection. A small child will play cheerfully and thoughtlessly with the flowers on its mother's coffin: it neither understands nor shares the grief of its father and elder brothers and sisters.'[3] Of course, it is impossible for the school to give the apprentice these personal, deep experiences – they can only come from life. But what it can do, and what Kerschensteiner thought it should do, is to *tell* him about life and to introduce him to aspects of history and literature which portray men in different situations and which are of such a kind as to inspire altruism. The educative value of historical studies, through which the pupils could be brought into contact with the first-rate, was also summed up by Sir Richard Livingstone as follows:

'Many things have conditioned and contributed to the ascent of humanity; biology, climate, economics have played a part; but so have great men. . . . It is on this side of history we must concentrate if we are looking for standards and values and the first-rate in human nature and conduct. The record of peoples and civilizations and the growth and decline of institutions and nations offer no doubt visions of greatness: Greece was more than Pericles, Rome than Caesar, Britain than Cromwell or Chatham or Pitt. But it is in the personalities of history that we see most clearly courage and persistence, desire for wisdom and devotion to good – the great positive forces of the world by which humanity has climbed from cave and forest into a clearer air.'[4]

Both Kerschensteiner and Sir Richard Livingstone share similar views on the role which history should play in schools. The Munich educator recognized the teaching of history in his continuation schools as being of primary significance for it provided the means by which he could bring his pupils into contact with men of greatness, who, born of different epochs and conditions, all showed one common factor – self-dedication to others and a display of moral courage. The pupil would be inspired by the nobility of soul which characterized these men. By introducing a historical survey of human advancement into the continuation schools, Kerschensteiner also intended to encourage in the pupil an understanding and insight into the laws which govern progress, and an insight into the composition of the community and of the State and the dependence of each citizen on the other. For only by giving the pupil a knowledge and comprehension of his fellow-beings and of their feelings and actions in a certain given

The Organization of the Schools · 57

situation – feelings and actions which could have been his own, if he himself had been placed in similar circumstances, was it possible for the pupil to set up bonds of sympathy between himself and his fellows and thus to welcome the coming of altruism.

But here some form of limitation had to be imposed, for a survey of the history of civilization was far too vast a topic for treatment in the continuation schools, since the allotment of hours caused necessary restrictions on the subject matter. Kerschensteiner again applied his principles concerning the value of holding the pupil's interest and proposed to broaden the pupil's experience of life and people by bringing him into contact with personalities who were connected with his egocentric interests – his trade. The civic lessons, into which the teaching of history was to be incorporated, were to concentrate mainly on giving the apprentice a brief historical survey of the development of his trade:

'I should like to look on our civics lessons as presenting a kind of history of civilization which emerges from the history of the particular trade, in which a boy is engaged. Every trade, every profession, has a history which extends from the simple conditions of the past, through the fluctuating fortunes of time to the complicated circumstances of the present. Here on this historic path, which, step by step, uncovers the ever-increasing interdependence and bonds between men and groups of trades and which demonstrates the gradual interweaving of interests between all professions, peoples, and states, the pupil best comes to realize the limits of his justified egoism and to understand the tasks which the State has to perform in order to protect the rights of each citizen.'[5]

A more detailed account of his plans for civic lessons is given in Kerschensteiner's prize essay:

'The majority of trades, and in particular that large group of trades connected with the applied arts, have a past rich in events and characteristic personalities. The life of the guilds in the Middle Ages, their exclusiveness and common interests, their flowering and decline, the benefits and disadvantages for the individual members of the trade, the collapse of manufactures after the Thirty Years' War, the gradual recovery and the new struggle in the nineteenth century – all these aspects of history contain a richness of incident, which doubtless has a strong attraction for the apprentice – even in the exceptional case of the apprentice who shows but slight interest in his trade. For history always has a fascination for young people. The teacher has very many opportunities of bringing into his teaching thrilling incidents which have occurred in the general history of our country and also has opportunities of revealing the ways in which the individual's interests are related to those of the State. There are many occasions on which he can point out to his pupils the principles which determine a sound national economy and can touch upon the points of the constitution and industrial legislature which the pupil can reasonably grasp.

'A similar way of dealing with civics, one which is especially suitable for schools in large industrial areas, is afforded by a study of the history of the factory worker in the nineteenth century. Here, special attention would be given to the relevant industry in which the youngster is employed. There are many events, which, properly treated, cannot fail to make an impression on the pupil. The youngster will come into contact with the exalting spectacle of courageous struggles all fought with trust in God, patriotism, human joy, and suffering, wherein outstanding individuals in our country play an active part. Examples come to hand of shining deeds of brotherly love, of the devotion of individual members of the clergy and laity to the poor and weak, of self-denial and perseverance. And, at the same time, there is continued progress, and the lot of those who are efficient and hard-working is continually improved. While studying these aspects of history we meet with the most vital social problems — questions concerned, for instance, with protection of labour, the organization of co-operative societies and trade unions, housing conditions, points of constitution and industrial law, commerce and communications. Then there are numerous subjects of a more general moral nature which come to light.'

Kerschensteiner's emphasis on the value of instruction in tools, materials, and raw products has already been mentioned, but deserves a fuller investigation at this point:

'A third way of giving civic instruction is directly connected with the instruction in practical work, tools, and products. . . . It arises from a study of the raw products, the manufacture or sale of which provides the youngster with his employment. For instance, in agricultural continuation schools, the civic instruction could be based on lessons on corn cultivation or cattle rearing – two subjects which will

The Organization of the Schools · 59

gain the immediate interest of country boys. The treatment of the growing of corn and the wage and salary structure of farmers, the development of agriculture and its significance in the pupil's own region will lead to a study of its national importance. After that one can go on to deal with agricultural conditions in the neighbouring European countries, and that leads on to a study of world corn production. Then corn trade and corn prices will be treated, followed by price changes and the legal and illegal means of price increasing. All the various aspects of the subject must be dealt with – the advantages and disadvantages of high cereal prices, duties in Germany, the men who have played a prominent role in this history. Other points to be included are a study of the interrelations between industry and agriculture, the significance of industry – both for itself and for the agriculturist, agricultural societies and their influence, commercial treaties and the bodies which conclude them, the Reich constitution and the local constitution and administration.'[6]

In this way, once the pupil's interest had been seized, the teaching of the history of the individual trades was to be extended and broadened so as to embrace a brief survey of the State and its functions. Here the pupil would be equipped with a basic knowledge of the form of the State and of his obligations, as a citizen, to that State.

To our shame, we English must note that Kerschensteiner was campaigning for a system of compulsory further education for all, which would provide the future generations with the knowledge and skills necessary for citizenship – and yet even now, in the second half of the twentieth century, we still insist on sending out the majority of our secondary modern school children at the age of fifteen to battle with life as best they can, alone, and with few hands to guide them. Just at the time when they are taking up employment for the first time, and are thus necessarily slowly becoming aware of the part which they and their employment play in the economic life of the country, and when they are acquiring an interest for national political life, we in England discontinue all compulsory education, and by so doing, we exclude them also from the possibility of receiving instruction in civics and current events, such as Kerschensteiner had in mind.

Yet, civic instruction, important as it was in the schools, was not the be-and-end-all of education, as Kerschensteiner well recognized. Among the more mature pupils civic instruction could, **at the most**, inspire altruism, but unless the schools gave some opportunity for altruistic action their purpose was nigh lost. Inspiring the pupils with altruistic thoughts alone was not enough – the proof of success lay in the performance of altruistic *deeds*. For the mature and more intellectually gifted pupils altruism would be recognized and increased by insight, but the majority of elementary and continuation school pupils did not yet possess this power of insight, and for them the change from egoism to altruism must be effected by a process of habit formation. The schools were to habituate these young people to work for the advantage of others, so that when the age of insight did appear, insight would take over the role of habit and the pupils would place themselves and their work joyfully in the service of their fellow men, conscious of the fact that, by so doing, they were furthering the progress both of the State, and of their fellow citizens. Kerschensteiner had already designated the primary tasks of the schools as being to ensure that the pupils acquired virtues such as diligence, determination, cleanliness, patience, and conscientiousness through habit formation; now he was determined that habit formation was also to be the means by which the schools diverted these virtues from egoistic to altruistic paths.

GROUP WORK

But how were the pupils best to be trained to take a responsible attitude towards their work, and to be satisfied only with work of quality? How were they to be trained to be motivated by altruism? How were they to be habituated to work with pleasure and dedication at tasks which they knew would benefit not only themselves but also, more important, the community? For Kerschensteiner the answer to all these questions was: in *group* work. Here the ultimate achievement of the work in hand was a common achievement; the only goal was a common goal. Kerschensteiner firmly believed that it was by giving the pupils this opportunity to work together at common tasks, that they would be habituated to be incited by altruistic thoughts and deeds.

Kerschensteiner's own special interest was directed to the introduction of group work into the practical lessons, which were to form a basic and integral part of the curriculum in his reorganized elementary and continuation schools:

'Everyone will grant, without further ado, that the workshops and laboratories in our Munich elementary and continuation schools can be excellent training grounds for the basic virtues such as accuracy, conscientiousness, carefulness, honesty, etc. . . . But these elementary virtues are not yet civic virtues, or, in other words, the virtues of moral self-assertion are generally not those of moral self-denial. The change over from the one to the other is effected when they are brought to use in the service of others. The invaluable advantage of practical work in the school laboratories, workshops, kitchens, and gardens lies in the fact that it can take on the form of joint work in a quite natural way. This is an advantage which is not usually shared by academic work.

'As soon as the pupils have acquired the requisite manual skills, usually in the second year of their apprenticeship, they can occasionally work on some larger project in groups, or even as a class. While they are all engaged on some common piece of work in this way they all experience common success and failure, and they all come to feel common joy in their work and common disappointments. The ambition of the individual must fit in with the ambition of the class. The achievement of the individual does not rise above that of the whole group. It is here in group work that a sense of responsibility for one's actions is developed, which is so important in later life and which is so painfully lacking here in Germany – not only among the ordinary people, but among the educated as well.

'By doing this type of work the individual learns how to subordinate himself to others and how to help his weaker and less talented companions. Here, too, he first comes to understand that his own interests can, and should, merge into the interests of others. The civic virtues of devotion and self-control grow out of this collective work, characterized by its well-thought-out plan and well-fitting order. Likewise, when the virtues of carefulness, conscientiousness, hard work, and perseverance are employed in common service they are transformed into altruistic virtues. This joint work provides, then, fruitful soil for civic instruction in such subjects as community life, its plan and order, the common tasks and duties in the employer's workshop, on the farm, in the parish, in the borough and in the State. This joint work is the character-forming foundation for civic instruction, which, however, is of no value to the majority of pupils, unless there is a simultaneous training of the will. As far as I know, this aspect of instruction in practical work has even been overlooked by the apostles of practical work.'[7]

Thus group work was not only important because it could give an ethical value to work but also because of the emphasis it could lay on the development of the social talents of its members. The study group was, in fact, a mirror of life itself, a community of people of different intelligences and interests, all necessarily interdependent, the one on the other. It was an excellent training ground for the development of human and social qualities which would be needed by the citizen in the larger town and State community.

OTHER APPLICATIONS OF GROUP WORK

It has been shown that Kerschensteiner conceived of practical work as presenting the most suitable basis for group activity. Indeed, he occupied himself very little with the possibilities of group work in the academic subjects. It is therefore interesting to note that despite his apparent lack of concern about details of the value of collective work among the more academic pupils, the study group – the 'Arbeitsgemeinschaft', as it is called in German – is now a permanent and well-established feature of normal Gymnasium routine in Germany. Here the pupils meet together often on a voluntary basis, once or twice a week, and, under the guidance of the teacher, pursue some joint project or topics for discussion arising from their school work, and, by so doing, help to develop that spirit of co-operation which Kerschensteiner intended his less-gifted pupils to develop through the pursuit of practical work.

In England, the outstanding example of successful group activity in the academic field is evident of course in the Sixth Form work undertaken in the grammar school. Here, the English are fortunate in having relatively small groups of pupils all working and discussing together academic topics, thus each contributing to the common pursuit of the discovery of knowledge. It is here, both in the individual and collective research required for the analysis of a subject, that the pupils experience true self-participation or ego-involvement – and in this experience they necessarily also achieve development, both of mind and of character.

An interesting experiment in group activity is being conducted in

The Organization of the Schools · 63

France too, where, since 1945 pilot classes have been introduced among eleven- to fifteen-year-olds in certain selected schools, which also base much of their teaching on activity methods and group work. The classes are organized in such a way that the teaching has one central theme common to all the subjects. Like Kerschensteiner's 'activity school', the French 'classes pilotes' are characterized by group work and activity methods, whereby measuring, drawing, modelling, etc., are essential features of the system.

RESPONSIBILITY

However, group work was not the only means by which Kerschensteiner intended to unfold the pupil's sense of responsibility towards his fellows, for there remained, too, the possibility of allotting to pupils various tasks of responsibility, which would normally be taken over by adults. Although this was an aspect of education which he considered to be of great benefit in the development of a true feeling of responsibility and community spirit, it is a feature of his work which has never been widely implemented in the German school system. In this respect, the English and American schools offer far more scope, the only German schools which offer similar kinds of facilities being the various 'Schullandheime' and boarding-schools.

The Schullandheim movement has now become widespread throughout Germany and there are two hundred and sixty-four such schools, usually situated in pleasant country surroundings, which are attended by classes from the ordinary compulsory schools, usually for periods of up to two weeks. During their stay in these schools, the youngsters learn to live and work together in a community, under the guidance of their teachers, and there can be no doubt that they offer an experience to the pupils, which is otherwise so rare in the German school system, where, even at university level, community life such as it is experienced on the English and American campus, is virtually unknown.[8]

If the pupils were to be trained to have a sense of responsibility towards the welfare of others, Kerschensteiner judged that it was essential for the schools to give them some opportunity whereby they could be engaged actively in useful service of their fellows. This opportunity was of course presented, to some extent, by the joint work on which the pupils were engaged, but there was also another way of actively involving the pupils in the interests of others. This was to be effected by giving them tasks of responsibility in the school, which would otherwise have been carried out by adults. Here, many jobs connected with the efficient organization and running of the school workshops could successfully he handed over to carefully chosen pupils.

The question of whether one could actually go farther than this, and award the pupils responsible tasks pertaining to the administration of school discipline and functions, was one which, however, caused Kerschensteiner some misgivings. He realized that pupil-involvement on this higher level demanded more exacting qualities and abilities from the pupil and that if this administration by the pupil were to be introduced into the continuation schools, then it would have to be introduced with the greatest caution.

Time has shown that, on the whole, administration by the pupil has not been incorporated into the German school system, not even into the academic Gymnasium, where the prefect system is still virtually unknown and where suggestions from any so-called pupil committee originate, to a large extent, from the teachers themselves.

From these considerations, which allow only brief mention here, it has been shown that Kerschensteiner understood the school's task as being far greater than just to produce skilled individuals. It was equally important that the school should be a place for the furtherance of the moral and social aspects of the child's development. At the time when he was reviewing the school system, the continuation schools played an indifferent role in education ('the general continuation school was an object of indifference to the pupils, was tedious to the masters and was a labour of love to the teachers, but all in vain')[9], and the pupils felt that they had no personal contact or feelings of loyalty towards them. This Kerschensteiner intended to change by raising the status of the schools.

First of all he planned to sever the continuation schools of all connexions with the elementary school and to make them schools in their own right. Then the quality and relevance of their work would be improved and the scope of their influence extended, so that the pupils would eventually be proud to attend them. The schools' tasks were no longer to be confined to the instruction of their pupils for a certain number of hours per week, but instead, the schools and teachers should offer pillars of moral support and guidance to their

The Organization of the Schools · 65

pupils as much as possible during non-teaching hours also. Many pupils obtained few stimuli, whether intellectual or moral, from their home background. This was especially the case among those who came from the growing industrial cities, where vice, immorality, and drinking were much in evidence. Kerschensteiner was convinced that the schools should provide facilities for the pupils' leisure time, whereby their interests and pursuits might be directed into more worthy channels.

Connected with their leisure pursuits, he envisaged the introduction of optional extra-curricular activities such as gymnastic clubs, excursion trips, school concerts, etc., such as had already been introduced in Leipzig by the celebrated educator, Oskar Pache. Unfortunately, these excellent beginnings never found widespread implementation because of a lack either of buildings or of interested teachers who were willing to undertake the extra work. Extra-curricular activities of many kinds are to be found within the modern vocational school system, but the enthusiasm for and extent of such ventures vary from school to school.

Far from the being concerned only with the reorganization of curricula, Kerschensteiner always occupied himself with the broader issues of education, for he recognized that the instruction given in schools could play only a very restricted part in the education of the people, in the face of such powerful environmental influences. He was a staunch campaigner in all the battles for social progress, whether they were fought for the improvement of housing conditions, or for an increase in the space allotted to public parks and playing fields. He took on extra duties in all fields of education and social welfare and was especially well known for his valuable work in promoting the spread of public libraries, museums, further education courses, child protection, and preservation of folklore.

WHAT FORM SHALL WORK TAKE?

Thus Kerschensteiner's new 'activity school' was to lay far more stress on the development of the child's social aptitudes than had hitherto been the case in German schools. He saw this aspect of education as being particularly important in the education of the unskilled workers. It has been shown also that Kerschensteiner conceived of independent, productive work as being a means of satisfying the soul's hunger for self-fulfilment and that therefore this work was to be placed at the centre of the teaching in his continuation schools.

There is, however, a restriction here. This conception of the value of work can be effected well enough in the training of craftsmen, who truly see their efforts helping to fashion a finished product, but it cannot be given the same validity in our modern, machine age with its vast body of unskilled workers, whose time is employed, for the main, on purely mechanical work where little skill is required and where all the necessary planning and thinking out has already been carried out by the higher personnel. In these unskilled jobs the work is of such a nature that it cannot possibly afford any real interest or ego-involvement to the worker employed in it. For workers such as these, whose numbers were already increasing in the large German cities, Kerschensteiner demanded that the continuation school should provide some other means whereby their life would be given a sense of purpose. Some suggested that religion, art, or knowledge would give the same fulfilment of soul which Kerschensteiner had intended to give through independent, productive work, but he himself rejected these suggestions as being insufficient in themselves, for he felt that a complete satisfaction and fulfilment of soul could only really be gained, not through knowledge or thoughts but through personal *action*.

One such sphere of action was immediately evident to Kerschensteiner, whereby the pupils could be engaged on creative, productive work and would thereby gain what Kerschensteiner termed 'content in life' (Lebensinhalt). He felt, namely, that the youngsters would gain a sense of purpose in life if they were given the opportunity to be involved in some kind of social work, which would be of benefit to their fellows. Kerschensteiner had in mind some kind of work, of which the system of 'mutualités scolaires' in Paris was an example. Here, the pupils all set aside a few centimes each week which were then distributed to needy children who required money for the payment of medical fees and other bills. In Dresden, too, another kind of social work was being undertaken by girls who volunteered to take on the task of supervising the many elementary school children at their sports sessions twice a week.

The problem of how to give a satisfactory education and purpose in life to the numerous juveniles employed in unskilled labour remains as large today as it was in Kerschensteiner's time. Several possibilities for solving this have been pointed out, such as 'education for leisure', the advocates of which demand that the youngsters should be given instruction in their hobbies and should be encouraged to take up new ones. Here, general lessons in art, music, handwork, gardening, etc., are indicated. Others propose that instead of educating youth to use its ever-increasing leisure time more wisely, we should insist that they receive some training for skilled employment. Neither of these proposals seems entirely satisfactory in itself, and it could well be that Kerschensteiner's theories, on the value of social work for the enrichment of the individual who undertakes it, offer a valid solution.

It is apparent with how much enthusiasm and vigour voluntary social work of all kinds, both at home and overseas, is tackled by young people. There is an ever-increasing number of volunteers wishing to join Voluntary Service Overseas, an organization which, to a certain extent, gained its inspiration from the splendid work of the American Peace Corps, and which enables the participants to dedicate one full year of their lives to community service abroad.[10] Opportunities for shorter periods of service in foreign countries are also available through the international work camps.

At home, much splendid community service is being undertaken by enthusiastic young people who are members of various organizations and institutions such as youth clubs, the Y.M.C.A., the scouts' and guides' movements, the Atlantic College, etc. The magnificent work of Mr Alec Dickson and his community service volunteers, who have undertaken work in so many varied and difficult fields, also deserves special praise. At some schools, too, voluntary service units have been established, whereby some proportionately short periods of school time may regularly be devoted to various kinds of social work. After suitable instruction or training, schoolchildren are able to supervise the road-crossing which their younger fellows use every day (this is a service which is commonly carried out by schoolchildren in Germany), to help old people with their housework, decorating, or gardening, to help in local hospitals, or to give assistance with the supervision of hobbies and leisure pursuits in orphanages or schools for the blind. Opportunities for the enthusiasm and idealism of youth to be channelled into community service, which can be performed both under official auspices and from individual initiative, are numerous and varied. Unfortunately, however, these opportunities are not always made apparent to and encouraged in young people. This was one of the points raised in a debate in the House of Lords on youth and social service:

'... we are failing in our generation to give these young people the example, the inspiration and the opportunities they need to enable them to display and use the enormous amount of good that they have inside them if only we can draw it out.'[11]

The opportunities for carrying out worthwhile, voluntary community service, wherein our youngsters may shape their character and gain a richness of soul, must be made available to all our youth. For it is in the pursuit of this type of work that they may become convinced of the principle which governed Kerschensteiner's own acts and deeds, namely, that: 'The purpose of life is not to rule, but to serve."[12]

6 · The Realization of His Plans

THE BEGINNINGS

The prize essay, which provided the kernel of his plans for further education, had made Kerschensteiner a famous man almost overnight, and by 1900 his detailed plans had been drawn up and approved on both local and ministerial level. The success of the venture was by no means assured however, for there still remained a great deal of restraint and even direct opposition among the ranks of the teachers and small employers. It was, of course, essential that their co-operation and enthusiasm be assured, if the new schools were to find widespread acceptance.

Then followed tired and anxious years for the Munich schools director, during which he travelled round from guild to guild, from one trade association to another, speaking to 'masters' and employers in an inspired effort to convince them of the inadequacy of existing facilities and of the need for systematic apprentice training in properly equipped schools. The basic hostility of the 'masters' was slow to change, for since the establishment of open competition they had ceased to feel any moral obligation towards the spiritual, moral, and educational welfare of their apprentices and saw them only from the materialistic viewpoint of 'usefulness'. Thus Kerschensteiner not only had to convert the 'masters' to accept the *form* of his schools but first of all had even to change their very attitude towards their apprentices.

As regards the form of the schools, his main task was to convince the 'masters' of the necessity for their apprentices to receive a threefold training; namely, a technical training which would ensure them the necessary technical or professional skills; secondly, training in business and economy (both of which were of great significance in the newly emerged economic state); and, thirdly, training in citizenship. The existing schools as they stood, he argued, could not possibly meet these demands, for they were either of the general type and thus competely ignored the educational opportunities presented by trade instruction, or were schools of a purely technical nature, such as the old trade schools or specialized technical schools, and concentrated purely on imparting vocational skills. Even the vocational education given in some of these old trade schools was far from satisfactory, for the teaching was based to a large extent on trade drawing, rather than on practical work, and thus sometimes could even drive a talented student out of his trade, transforming an efficient joiner into a mediocre furniture designer.

FOREIGN ACHIEVEMENTS

The importance of this field of practical work in schools had impressed itself on Kerschensteiner's mind particularly during his extensive investigations and school inspections, both abroad and in other parts of Germany, the results of which he published in 1901.[1] For instance, the achievements of the Austrian trade schools (Handwerkerschulen), of which Germany possessed no corresponding equivalent, afforded him a special interest. These schools were attended by children of the sixth elementary school class, who were therefore about twelve years of age. A course lasting from two to three years was offered, which provided further elementary school education combined with a firm basis of technical training. In the first class, the handwork taught was of a general nature, half the year being devoted to metalwork and the other half to woodwork. In the second class, the pupils were split up into trade classes and the teaching became more specialized. The apprentice workshops of Bern in Switzerland also gained Kerschensteiner's approval, in the main, although they lacked the teaching in economics and civics which was an essential feature of the French training schools.

It was clear that Munich urgently had to reconsider the whole question of further education, if it was not to be left behind other towns in this matter. Yet, at the same time, Kerschensteiner pointed out that the authorities and employers were to proceed with caution and should not be misled into taking over entire foreign systems and transplanting them heedlessly on to Bavarian soil. Some of the foreign systems had obvious advantages, but practically all of them had defects too. For instance, Kerschensteiner judged that the Austrian and Swiss schools which he had seen, although greatly surpassing the Munich facilities for technical training, concentrated far too much on the training of the worker. They disregarded the training of the *man*, and it was precisely this aspect of education which should form the basis of all school organization.

THE REACTION TO HIS PROPOSALS

Much opposition was raised to the very central theme of Kerschensteiner's philosophy, namely, that all further education should take place on the basis of trade instruction. Indeed, this battle between the advocates of vocational education, on the one hand, and those of general education, on the other, has been waged ever since. In England the champions of general education have gained the upper hand, and sit back in satisfaction at the idea of our youth being compelled to stay yet one more year at school, till the age of sixteen, having a 'general education' pumped into them, which they neither appreciate nor want.[2] Concerning this point, Kerschensteiner could not do better than quote the words of Goethe in his *Wilhelm Meisters Wanderjahre* – 'to know and to practise one thing well has a greater educative value than to have a smattering of a hundred.'[3]

With regard to the raising of the compulsory school-leaving age, Kerschensteiner felt that no useful purpose would be served by an extension of the elementary school in its existing form. The only satisfactory way of extending compulsory education was to insist on compulsory continuation school attendance among all youngsters engaged in apprenticeships in skilled trades. Only here would the education be the most effective, where the way of education, the professional training, was closely bound to the needs and realities of life. An extension of the ordinary elementary school should only be considered for unskilled workers, and even then the extra elementary school teaching should bear a closer connexion with life and should attempt to prepare the pupils for entry into skilled work later.[4] On the whole, Germany has thought well in the years that were to follow, to adopt Kerschensteiner's suggestions: the elementary school leaving age is fifteen and in one or two states even remains at fourteen, while compulsory vocational school attendance is universal – for all youngsters, whether they are engaged in skilled or unskilled work.

The other aspect of Kerschensteiner's new scheme which aroused heated controversy, especially among the 'masters', was the importance which Kerschensteiner assigned to practical work in his schools. The reader will remember that efficient workshop instruction was one of the fundamental axioms of Kerschensteiner's vocational education. Not only was it to be fused organically into the curriculum but, even more important, it was to form the very basis for the acquisition of all new theoretical knowledge and for the formation of those qualities of character requisite of social man. Also, since all true education was self-education, practical work was essential in the schools: it provided the means by which the child could learn by discovery, by thoughtful trial and error, by observation and comparison, by experience. Active practical work was the sap, the life food for the blossoming of self-education.

The strong opposition to Kerschensteiner's demand for the introduction of practical work gave proof of just how little the essentials of Kerschensteiner's ideas and philosophy had really been grasped and understood. The 'masters' and small employers, in particular, strongly criticized the introduction of practical work on the grounds that the apprentice was engaged in practical work all day long and that the small amount of handwork accomplished in school could provide but little opportunity for the apprentice to obtain any new or worthwhile skills. They saw their own training as being thoroughly adequate and competely disregarded the educational aspects of practical work.

The high costs for the implementation of Kerschensteiner's proposals also caused great concern. His workshop instruction demanded the building of well-equipped workshops, fitted out with all the necessary tools and machinery for the various trades – a project which would cause a heavy drain on local funds. It was a mark of Kerschensteiner's character that he would be satisfied only with the best, and this same teacher, who had refused to teach biology in Schweinfurt until he himself was a complete master of the subject, now insisted that his new schools were to have only first-rate buildings and equipment and first-rate teachers, if the education offered in them was to be successful. His teachers were not to be mere dilettantes in matters of technical education but were to be given courses of training, which would ensure that they were well qualified to teach the theoretical subjects with pedagogical insight.[5] The workshop instruction was to be left entirely in the hands of qualified and experienced 'masters' and skilled workmen who would be drafted in from the various trades and professions. High quality in the teaching was essential.

This proposal to bring 'manual workers' into the schools caused great distress in the ranks of the solid, status-conscious teachers; indeed, many of them were appalled at the step, which they were sure would jeopardize the dignity and the prestige of the teaching profession.

LINKING THE SCHOOLS WITH INDUSTRY

So it was to the trade associations that Kerschensteiner turned for help in his enterprise, for he realized that their support was vital to his new trade-specialized continuation schools. He also planned to give them a close liaison with the schools, thereby providing that link between school and trade which was necessary if the schools were to be organized along modern and efficient lines, and if the maximum benefit was to be gained from the instruction. He described these early efforts and trials in a speech he made in 1902:

'... above all I aimed at reawakening an interest in educational tasks among "masters" in the same trade group. In almost every group there still exists a certain amount of community feeling . . . which is expressed when a small or large number of "masters" in the same trade meet together to look after their common interests and to form guilds, associations, unions, clubs, or societies, through which they can represent their views. I tried to give these associations a new centre of interest, and endeavoured to arouse an enthusiasm for the education of the youngsters engaged in their own trade. I not only pointed out the means but I also strove to help them cultivate this new sphere of interest. . . . The natural consequence of this plan was to drop the general continuation school and to put in its place the specialized-trade continuation school. For I could only expect an association to be interested in a continuation school which gave specialized classes in its own particular trade.

'The demand for a specialized-trade continuation school is of course not new. Among the German states Baden's trade schools had taken the lead with the organization of their teaching in groups of trades and, among the large German towns, Leipzig had already introduced trade specialization on a large scale. . . . But the new aspect of my school organization was that, as far as possible, the *individual trade* was to be at the centre of the teaching. However, the most striking innovation in these public and locally maintained schools was that with each individual trade-specialized school I connected a relevant trade association. This was brought about by allowing the trade association to play a part in the organization and inspection of the schools. The trade association was also to put forward efficient "masters" or skilled workers as salaried teachers. Moreover, it also paid for the materials used in the practical instruction and provided models for the drawing lessons, while the municipality undertook the provision of buildings, teachers' salaries, teaching aids, machines, and tools.'[6]

The first trade associations to prove amenable and to lend their active co-operation were those of the butchers, bakers, cobblers, barbers, hairdressers and wig-makers, and chimney-sweeps. The success of schools which specialized in these trades was immediate and soon led to the eager founding of other schools. The good report of these schools spread from trade to trade, and any misgivings which the 'masters' might have harboured against the schools gradually disappeared, as they became converted by their own apprentices' enthusiasm. The number of schools rapidly increased so that in 1902 Kerschensteiner had 22 of them, 40 in 1906, and 46 in 1907. By 1912 there were 54 such schools, or courses, as we would now term them, which were accommodated in 8 buildings in Munich, with a total of 534 teachers and 9,284 pupils.

DETAILS OF THE ORGANIZATION OF THE NEW SCHOOLS

The years of energy and effort were at last bearing fruit and, thanks to his own complete and entire devotion to the cause, and to the unfailing support and hard work of those few self-sacrificing 'masters' and skilled workmen who had so willingly offered their services in those first years, Kerschensteiner was gradually and steadily able to transform the old 'bookish' general continuation school into a place pulsating with enthusiasm, an 'activity school'.

In accordance with his earlier demands, the teaching in his new schools was put forward to the day-time. A common arrangement was for the student to attend from 4 to 7 p.m. on one day, and from 2 to 6 p.m. on another. Any other necessary lessons were then given on a Sunday morning. The organization of the teaching hours was arranged as much as possible to fit in with the circumstances and conditions of the individual trades: for instance, trades with seasonal work were able to send their apprentices in the 'off-season'. Thus, apprentices in the building trade, dock-workers and decorators, for instance, attended the specialized-trade continuation school for twelve hours per week during the winter months and in the summer months had only three hours' instruction per week. In the same way, other trades of a seasonal nature had a fuller timetable for eight or nine months instead of attending the full school year of ten months – for example, youngsters working in such trades as photography, jewellery, and confectionery did not attend school during the month of December, when their full-time services would be required at their place of employment.

At first, many of Kerschensteiner's schools had to be accommodated in elementary school buildings, but, in time, new central buildings became available. At the beginning of 1907 compulsory attendance at continuation school came into force in Munich. This meant that boys engaged in some kind of skilled work now had to attend Kerschensteiner's new trade-specialized continuation schools until they reached the age of eighteen. Specialized trade classes had to be set up as soon as the number of apprentices in a particular trade rose to twenty.

But compulsory attendance at continuation school was by no means restricted to those youngsters who were employed in skilled trades and whose number reached a minimum of twenty. The obligation to attend a continuation school was imposed on all youngsters alike, irrespective of whether they were employed as apprentices in a skilled trade or in a smaller trade group with fewer apprentices, or in unskilled labour. Even if they were unemployed they still had to attend a continuation school. For all these varying groups of youngsters Kerschensteiner devised and set up a new non-trade specialized continuation school, which they were to attend for a period of two years.

Although this was a school offering a more general type of education, it was organized on completely different lines from the old nineteenth-century general continuation school. The curriculum was composed of the following subjects: religion, composition and reading, arithmetic, hygiene and civics, gymnastics (or athletics or swimming), wood- and metal-work and drawing. This kind of school enabled these boys to enjoy a prolonged general education, and at the same time the inclusion of practical work in the timetable was designed to encourage them to take up some kind of skilled occupation. The importance of the lessons in hygiene was one of the new aspects of education which Kerschensteiner had presented in his prize essay several years before. He judged it essential for all youngsters to be taught cleanliness and bodily care so that they might gain some insight into the rules of healthy living. He had also long since been a champion of gymnastics in schools, which he valued not only for their training of body but also for the immense role which they could play in character training – an idea which was only just receiving attention in German education.

These new general continuation schools formed a kind of extension to the ordinary elementary school, where significant developments were also taking place. Kerschensteiner was determined to make the elementary schools correspond more to the necessities and requirements which life would demand of these youngsters, and, with this end in view, he introduced practical work into the final optional class of the elementary school, a class which his predecessor had started in

1894. With the inclusion of practical work the attendance at this optional class immediately soared, and in 1907, after a trial period, Kerschensteiner could finally make the eighth school year compulsory (i.e. up to the age of fourteen). From this time onwards, about half the teaching time in this final class was devoted to practical work of some kind. Physics and chemistry, both with practical laboratory work, had now also been included in the elementary school curriculum. With regard to the training of girls, the change had been effected a little more slowly. The optional eighth class, with its emphasis on housekeeping, clothing, child care, nutrition, and other practical subjects received official sanction in 1896; but it was not made compulsory until 1913. The introduction of practical work in the elementary schools had a dynamic and far-reaching effect, for, whereas in 1890 one third of Munich's elementary school leavers had taken up unskilled, 'dead-end' jobs, by 1908 only $2\frac{1}{4}$ per cent of them were entering this kind of employment.

The Munich system of vocational education soon obtained such reputation that similar schools were set up by other German states in the following decade, although regulations regarding the length of attendance varied from state to state. Technical and vocational education came to assume a national importance and in 1908 there was founded the German Executive for the Technical School System which was to investigate the demands and requirements of industry with regard to the supply of young trained workers. This committee was to have the utmost importance for the development of technical education in Germany, as its scope and sphere of activity increased.

Kerschensteiner's own reorganization of the Munich system of further education was virtually completed by 1914, by which time he had moulded the schools into places teeming with zest and industry, where the sixty workshops, which were at their disposal, were designed to accommodate no more than sixteen to twenty students at any one time. In addition to the compulsory teaching, optional excursions and evening meetings directed the students' leisure-time interests into worthy channels.

The curriculum followed the principles expressed in his earlier work; for instance, the curriculum for mechanics was organized on the following lines:

	Hours per week			
	Cl 1	Cl 2	Cl 3	Cl 4
Religion	1	1	1	–
Arithmetic and bookkeeping	1	1	1	1
Business essay and reading	1	1	1	–
Civics and hygiene	1	1	1	1
Trade drawing	3	2	3	3
General physics	2	–	–	–
Mechanics and electrotechnics with practical work	–	3	2	4
Total hours	9	9	9	9
Voluntary practical work	–	4	4	4

Within so few years Kerschensteiner had succeeded in completely reshaping the whole continuation school pattern in Munich, and had introduced a system which took into consideration not only the intellectual development of the pupils but also their practical and social bents. The threefold aspect of the curriculum – with its stress on technical skills, economic insight, and civic thinking, was designed to help train the true citizen, the formation of whom should be the ultimate aim of all democratic education.

A REFORM OF ART TEACHING

However huge and time-demanding the task of the school reorganization had been, Kerschensteiner nevertheless still found time and energy to occupy himself with matters concerning other aspects of education. A reform of the teaching of art was one of these ideas which had preoccupied him for a considerable period of time, for he considered the existing system in no way encouraged the child's natural ability. Art was, of course, an established subject in the German elementary schools and instruction in drawing had also taken a prominent position in the curriculum of the old trade schools. Along with music, art still remained one of Kerschensteiner's own hobbies.

For six years he collected and studied half a million drawings executed by Munich elementary school children; pressure of work weighed so heavily on him that he scarcely found time to meet with his own family. He had set out to study the artistic ability in the child and his attitude and relation to art, with a view to establishing the means by which the child's artistic gifts might best be developed. His conclusions were published in 1905 in a book of colossal magnitude,[7] which was the prelude to a complete reorganization of the principles of art teaching.

His views on the role of art in schools, and the methods of teaching it, raised much criticism among the teaching profession. Kerschensteiner did not subscribe to the view that in every child there was a dormant artistic genius which would express itself as soon as the child was given systematic instruction in art. He considered that, instead, it was enough if the child came to derive pleasure from drawing and painting and pursued art for its own sake. Kerschensteiner was also doubtful of the view currently held, that artistic work would lead to moral ennoblement. In 1903 as chairman of the conference on art education, held in Weimar, he quoted the aims of art teaching as being to increase the pupil's power of self-expression, to awaken an understanding for artistic expression, and, finally, to bring the child to appreciate and enjoy art, the last-mentioned being a very difficult task to accomplish.

Along with all the other subjects in Kerschensteiner's curriculum, art was to be incorporated as part of the scaffolding of civic education. Kerschensteiner considered that one of the most important features of art education was that, through it, the child would be trained and habituated to *observe* closely and attentively. This power of thoughtful observation and the ability to grasp the essential and characteristic feature of any given object and to assess a situation were qualities which could be trained in art lessons, and were qualities vital to the good citizen who was to play an effective part in the State. One of the most significant tasks of education was the development of the power of observation and this could be effected especially well in the art and science lessons, where observation was the very basis on which personal experience was founded.

Art, too, satisfied the child's inclination towards productive self-activity: it was the expression of the child's creative urge and, as such, was to be encouraged and furthered. At the same time, art could be streamed into *useful*, productive channels, thus fulfilling the educative demands of all true and worthy practical work in schools.

The Realization of His Plans · 79

Kerschensteiner's art syllabus for the elementary school bore marked differences from what was being taught at that time. For instance, he planned to introduce systematic instruction in drawing only in the fifth school year. The main difference, however, between Kerschensteiner's art teaching and that of his contemporaries was that Kerschensteiner was determined to avoid all the geometric drawing which was so typical a feature of contemporary art instruction. Instead of this geometrical drawing, Kerschensteiner concentrated much more on drawing from memory objects which had previously been shown, studied, and discussed. Later on in the instruction, models would be copied and then, in the top class, the use of perspective would be studied.

These new proposals met with the usual cold hostility, which was by now the customary reaction to any plans connected with the name of Kerschensteiner. At an exhibition of Munich schoolchildren's work, harsh protests were raised against the lowering of artistic standards which was apparently evident in the 'poster-like' paintings, which, the critics judged, had been painted by children who had obviously not been allowed to follow their own artistic bents and inclinations. Yet, despite the tide of criticism against him, Kerschensteiner continued to put his aims into practice and succeeded in awarding to art a more important place in school, not only as an independent subject in the curriculum but also as an auxiliary means of illustrating other subjects.

THE VALUE OF THE SCIENCES

Another subject to which Kerschensteiner drew the attention of German educationists was science. Whereas instruction in the sciences is now firmly established in the modern school system, when Kerschensteiner took up his new post at the end of the last century the teaching of science and allied subjects was not yet on a sound foundation. When Kerschensteiner had undertaken to give instruction in biology in Schweinfurt he was the only biology teacher in Bavaria. Physics and chemistry had already been introduced into the secondary schools since the 1850s, but when he had inspected the schools, Kerschensteiner had found the teaching to be dull and uninspired.

Kerschensteiner concluded from his observations that the methods employed in the teaching of science were similar to those used in other school subjects, namely, that the pupils discussed, wrote about, and read books on the subject concerned, but never came to grips with the subject through personal experience. Experiments were unknown. Kerschensteiner therefore campaigned vigorously for the introduction of laboratories and practical work in science teaching, for one of the principles essential to his pedagogical philosophy was that all practical work, whether it took place in scientific tests in the laboratory or at the workshop bench, was a vital force in the building of character and in the training of good working habits. In 1907 Kerschensteiner was able to introduce four lessons of physics and chemistry, including laboratory work, into the curriculum of the eighth class of the elementary school. Seven years previously he had already introduced into the same class six lessons per week of instruction in wood- and metal-work.

By his insistence on the place which the sciences deserved and should occupy in the curriculum, Kerschensteiner showed himself to be one of the pioneers of 'modern' education, although many of his views touching on the value of the sciences can no longer be acceptable to modern educational thought. His views as expressed in his work, *The Character and Value of the Sciences*,[8] published in 1914, represented the theory that a study of the sciences was valuable chiefly for its ability to train the mind to follow a logical, precise, and clear process of thought. From there, Kerschensteiner assumed that the mental discipline acquired by a study of the sciences could automatically be brought into play in any other field of thought. This view is, of course, contrary to modern views on the transfer of training from one subject to another.[9]

In addition to the training of mental discipline[10] which Kerschensteiner thought would be effected by scientific studies, he also held the sciences in high esteem for what he judged to be their ability to further the power of observation in the student. By observation he understood, of course, not merely the ability to notice and to perceive but the ability to judge and to appraise an object or a situation with a perfect objectivity, which allowed of no human bias. Observation, for Kerschensteiner, meant the combination of perception plus thought. The sciences were valuable here, because the whole of scientific study was based on a detached observation, where subjective judgements could play no part, for each stage of the examination or analysis had to be verified with logic and calculation. Art, too, could be of benefit in the development of the observation, as has already been shown.

The Realization of His Plans · 81

A third value of scientific studies was their ability to give the student an insight into the natural forces which determine all kinds of life, whatever form they may take on. Through a study of these subjects the student would learn to recognize the laws which govern health and growth. Also, with regard to this matter, Kerschensteiner was anxious to see that lessons in hygiene were given a regular place in the curriculum of the continuation schools.

THE SPREAD OF HIS IDEAS

Since the time when Kerschensteiner's plans for the reorganization of the continuation school system had been approved, new councillors had come into office who were unfriendly to their Director of Education, and once more Kerschensteiner's image became veiled in doubt and suspicion. He was a lonesome figure braving the storms of mistrust and criticism, and, during this period when Munich chose not to honour him, he received his encouragement from abroad. Munich was suddenly besieged by foreign educators and government representatives, who all came to pay homage to this man who had brought about such fundamental changes in education in so short a space of time.

He was deeply moved and proud of the honour bestowed on him when he was called to Zürich in 1908 to speak at the Pestalozzi anniversary celebrations, for Pestalozzi had always held a special and revered place in his heart. His speech in the Church of St Peter was one of passion and sincerity and betrayed a strong awareness of the nearness of the great master himself. It was a speech which had a profound impact on the educational world, for in it Kerschensteiner explained once more the principle underlying the foundation of the 'activity school'. The reaction to the speech was quick and biting. The phrase 'activity school' was soon bandied about among educationists and aroused scathing criticism. Kerschensteiner now found that his speech had been widely misunderstood and misinterpreted, and that his critics were condemning the concept of the 'activity school' without realizing the educational aims behind the scheme. Their eyes alighted only on the outer shell, not penetrating to the real significance of the schools.

In their dim vision his adversaries saw only a school which had a bias towards 'manual' work – that most lowly of occupations. They also found nothing to commend the group work, which was such an essential feature of this new type of school. They did not share Kerschensteiner's view that group work was an admirable means of giving youngsters the opportunity of working together in a small community, in which each and every one of them could develop his own talents and personality, and could learn to help his weaker and less-gifted classmates. Instead, these outspoken critics of innovation argued that group work could only result in the subordination of the group to their leader, who would then become complacent with feelings of superiority and self-satisfaction. They also ignored the fact that the activity school's principle of learning by doing was what Pestalozzi himself would have wished. The new features such as the acting of historical events, the making of models for use in history and geography, the weighing and measuring in the mathematics lessons all pointed, in their eyes, to a 'play school' where little real *work* was accomplished.

These next years were the most difficult for Kerschensteiner because of the unceasing criticism directed against him in his native Bavaria. Yet, at the same time, they were years of consolation too. In the same year as his controversial Zürich speech, Kerschensteiner undertook his first foreign lecture tour, which was to Scotland, where he was loudly acclaimed. Very soon followed tours in Hungary, Sweden, Holland, Russia, Denmark, Austria, and the Balkans, in which he outlined the Munich system with the same vigour which he had displayed on the soil of his own country.

Despite the strain of these tours Kerschensteiner gained an immense amount of satisfaction from them, which cheered his depressed spirit, for everywhere his views met with enthusiastic approval. The tours also provided an excellent opportunity for him to come into contact with foreign educationists with whom common problems could be discussed. His thirst for knowledge and experience was insatiable. His trip to America in 1910 left a deep and lasting impression on him, for there he experienced a different way of life and new educational forms which Europe did not know: schools containing thousands of pupils, all kinds of extra-curricular activities, school clubs of every nature, debating societies, well-equipped school libraries and laboratories, school magazines and school councils. Here, also, he made the acquaintance of Dewey's works, and was surprised to see how similar some of Dewey's ideas were to his own.

On his return home, he found, to his regret, that his views were still being misrepresented, and that even some of his foreign admirers regarded his system of vocational education purely from the utility point of view. Tired of all the misunderstandings which had veiled the true import of his ideas, he put pen to paper and, in the next few years, produced a series of books in which he set out his ideas in greater detail. In 1901 his prize essay[11] had been published, and in 1907 had appeared a collection of speeches and essays on school organization.[12] In the following year an outline of the Munich system[13] had been published, and also in the same year had appeared a sequel to his prize essay.[14] In 1912 appeared his book on character,[15] and also in the same year he published *The Concept of the Activity School*;[16] in this he gave detailed practical examples of the methods to be used in the activity schools, with special reference to elementary schools. He had already set up experimental pilot classes, using these methods, in the Munich elementary schools.

THE EDUCATION OF GIRLS

One aspect of further education which caused Kerschensteiner particular distress, was the existing poor facilities for the continued education of women. Compulsory attendance at the old Sunday (or Wednesday) classes had of course existed for all girls aged thirteen to sixteen since the beginning of the nineteenth century. However, although the teaching in these schools was reorganized in 1905 in Bavaria, when the three hours per week became devoted to the more 'useful' subjects of housewifery, arithmetic, reading, and writing, education for women still lay far behind that for men. Emancipation of women had not yet been effected, but Kerschensteiner demanded that before it was achieved, women must be equipped with a suitable education: they, too, would then have to vote and must know how to use it. Traditionally, woman's role had been that of wife and mother and she had not seemed important enough to warrant a good or extensive education. But Kerschensteiner's whole philosophy of education for women was based on the theory that, by entrusting the rearing of children and the making of a home to women, we were allotting them a role of inestimable importance in the nation's life:

'It is not true that the elementary school is or ever can be the educator of the people. That is one of those overestimations which cause us to overlook completely the fact that the first and foremost educators are the millions of families; the next educator is life in the community itself, and the school as an educational institution ranks only in third place.'[17]

Kerschensteiner's plans for the reorganization of the existing general continuation schools for girls were to have as their aim the training of girls to take up their natural role of wife and mother. Accordingly, the teaching was to be divided into three broad divisions: firstly, home-running; secondly, the educational duties of the mother; and thirdly, the duties and position of woman in the State. The curriculum was composed of the following subjects: religion, housekeeping and hygiene, German, accounts and domestic bookkeeping, and the training of children. Optional subjects were needlework (which had already been studied fairly extensively in the elementary school), French, English, and technical drawing. Visits were to be arranged to orphanages, homes for the deaf, dumb, or blind. Mothers' evenings were to he held, where the students would have the opportunity of meeting and talking with mothers, and visits would be made to local kindergartens where the students would be able to practise the games and read the fairy stories, and other material which they had collected.

For those girls employed in commerce, a commercial section was set up which would equip them with the knowledge and skills required in their employment. In 1914 it was also planned to increase the scope of the school by adding a trades section. A few months before the outbreak of the First World War attendance at a continuation school was made compulsory for all girls in Munich aged fourteen to sixteen who were not attending some other institution of higher education.

THE EDUCATION OF THE RURAL YOUTH

While the reorganization of the continuation schools went ahead with more vigour in Munich itself than in the remote country areas, Kerschensteiner also did much to improve the situation for the many agricultural workers who had no opportunity of attending a specialized-trade continuation school.

For the girls, too, he conceived the idea of the rural continuation school, whose curriculum was based mainly on domestic subjects but also included some elements of small farming.[18] The domestic instruction in the girls' schools dealt with such varied subjects as foods, hygiene, clothing and housing, baby care, children's games. Practical work (in the form of cookery and sewing) was also to constitute an essential part of the curriculum. The lessons in arithmetic and German were to be linked as much as possible with housekeeping – for instance, the arithmetic was based on calculations regarding fuel costs, food costs, costs of keeping a child, etc. The German lessons, which consisted of written and oral work, dealt with such subjects as letter writing, cookery recipes, orders, invoices, receipts, official forms. Where circumstances permitted and where the necessary experienced teaching staff was available, instruction was to be given in plant and animal care and in such topics as growing and pickling vegetables, the flower garden, poultry-keeping, and marketing.

The rural continuation schools for girls mostly only offered about five hours' instruction per week. Today, a similar type of school is widely attended in the agricultural South. On the whole, the rural schools have been much slower to develop than the trades or commercial schools, for it was not until the economic depressions of the 'twenties and 'thirties, that their true value was realized.

In Kerschensteiner's time, of course, the agricultural worker was still very much regarded as being a 'country yokel' of little natural wit. By introducing agricultural continuation schools for boys Kerschensteiner intended to prove that *all* men had in them the germs of true citizenship, irrespective of their social or economic background. Indeed, Kerschensteiner said that, with regard to education for citizenship, agricultural work had several advantages over other forms of employment, because, firstly, it was no mere job, in the lowest sense of the word, but was a life-giver, a means of preserving our civilization and heritage and, secondly, it carried with it an independence and self-reliance such as were afforded by no other vocation. Work and home life were fused into harmony, the whole family helping in the common task and, 'Since every kind of group work . . . unfolds considerable educative powers in the field of civics, one can say that no trade offers better possibilities for civic education than the agricultural trade.'[19]

Following the basic principle of Kerschensteiner's philosophy, namely, that efficient citizenship began with efficient work, so training in agriculture was to form the basis of the curriculum. Practical work was of course a characteristic of the instruction, and the students would study such subjects as: fruit-growing and bee-keeping, hygiene and civics, which included a history of agriculture. The boys were to gain a broader outlook and deeper interest in the wider application of ideas through discussions on topics both of local and national interest. As in all the other specialized-trade schools, the arithmetic was to be connected with the trade, and in the agricultural schools this would deal with balancing accounts, heating and lighting costs, mortgages, costs, profits, employees' insurance, rates, taxes, income, and expenditure of a moderate-sized farm. Reading practice would be taken both from the textbook and from the German classics. Written work would mostly be in the form of business letters.

Kerschensteiner's brilliant work in Munich served as an example to the rest of Germany of what could be achieved in the realm of vocational education. Compulsory attendance at existing continuation schools was reiterated repeatedly on the local level, and in the provisions of the 1919 Weimar Constitution compulsory continuation school attendance was finally extended to all Germany. The Reich Compulsory School Attendance Law of 1938 reaffirmed the compulsory attendance at these schools of all those youngsters who were not engaged in any other form of recognized education, whether they were in skilled or unskilled employment. Responsibility for the continued education of those young people aged between fourteen and eighteen was now handed over to the individual states.

Thus Kerschensteiner's aim that Germany should have a system of compulsory continued education, beyond that of the basic schooling, is now a well-established principle in modern Germany. The form of the modern schools will be discussed in the following chapter.

7 · The Modern German Vocational Schools

THE POST-WAR SITUATION

The 1939-45 war brought the entire education system in Germany into complete and utter chaos: by the end of the war all schooling was virtually at a standstill, with large numbers of buildings either completely or partially destroyed. When schooling was finally taken up again, necessity forced it to be run on a shift basis. The tremendous task of rebuilding was undertaken after the currency reform of 1948, but, despite the enormous output of new buildings, it was not until well on in the 1950s that sufficient progress had been made for a recognizable pattern of vocational school education to emerge. But lack of buildings and facilities were not the only difficulties which faced the re-establishment of the educational system. In addition to these deficiencies, there was an acute shortage of teachers, many of whom had either fallen in the war or had been dismissed from their posts immediately after the war in the systematic denazification of the schools which had been undertaken by the allies.

The structure of the modern German vocational schools testifies to the wide-reaching influence and success of Kerschensteiner's work in the field of further education. Kerschensteiner justifiably earned himself the title of 'father of the vocational school', in the same way as his revered Pestalozzi had come to be called the 'father of the elementary school'. Kerschensteiner's principle that it was the task of the continuation school, or the vocational school, as it is now called, to help in the formation of a rounded personality, a person who was of firm and noble character, governed by high moral principles, whose talents and aptitudes were sufficiently developed to enable him to play his role efficiently in the community, both in a professional and non-professional capacity, is well in evidence in the modern vocational school system in Germany. This is shown quite clearly in the following extracts taken from the directives of one of the German states, where the aims of vocational school education are quoted as being: 'To give vocational training and to train the student to be a citizen who is conscious of his responsibilities and who is a moral personality: these tasks are of equal importance'.[1]

Kerschensteiner's precept that not general teaching, but trade instruction, should form the foundation of vocational school education, has now been put into practice throughout the whole of Germany. Every day hundreds of thousands of German youngsters attend the vocational schools, of which there are 2,300 in the Federal Republic, where they receive both practical and theoretical instruction in their trade. This instruction enables them to perform their daily work confidently and efficiently, thus ensuring for themselves the means to an independent and useful life in the community. A certain amount of teaching of a general or cultural nature is also an established feature of the schools.

CIVIC TEACHING

There is, however, one aspect of the present vocational school's teaching which has veered away from the lines which Kerschensteiner had intended. This is the teaching in civics. Kerschensteiner had planned the civic teaching to grow naturally out of the trade instruction and trade history. However, this has but very rarely been put into practice, and civic 'instruction' in the vocational schools has come to be a subject in its own right, with its own separate place allotted to it in the curriculum. Although its form is different from what Kerschensteiner himself had envisaged, it is nevertheless an established and recognized subject in the vocational school curriculum. On its educational value, one of the states says:

'The instruction in civics awakens a sense of responsibility among the pupils towards their immediate environment. The youngsters gain an insight into the moral order of life in a community and acquire a respect for human rights. They become conscious that all of them together bear a responsibility for the whole and this enables them to see the place they occupy in society, which they can then consciously take up. And so, in this way, the ground is prepared for experiences which are fruitful ethically and which form the basis of later political judgements. It is from such a frame of mind as this, that is born a love of one's own people and country, as well as an understanding for the rights of all peoples.'[2]

Civic instruction plays an essential role in the modern German vocational schools and the following syllabus (that for the state of Baden-Württemberg) gives an idea of the subjects and topics studied in these lessons by the 80 per cent of all German youngsters who pass through these schools.

FIRST YEAR

THE YOUNGSTER IN THE FAMILY, AT WORK AND IN PUBLIC

Dignity, self-appraisal, the importance of the person and his contact with the community.
Relations between parents, children, and brothers and sisters.
Survey of the vocational school system.
Facilities for further education.
Forms and aims of the youth societies and clubs.
Dangers existing for young people.

FORMS AND RULES FOR LIVING TOGETHER

Mutual understanding and dependence on one another at home, in school, at work, and in public.
Conduct and behaviour.

MEANS OF POLITICAL INFORMATION

Formation of public opinion under the influence of newspapers, journals, books, films, radio, television, and forums.
Propaganda and agitation.
Opinion polls and research into them.

THE POLITICAL COMMUNITIES IN THE LOCALITY

The natural home of people, making a new home in another part of the country, loss of native country.
History and economy of the locality and of the country as a whole. Town and country, preservation of nature and national monuments.
The organization of urban districts, rural districts, etc.
The importance of administration in parish and rural councils.
Current topics, remembrance days, revision.

SECOND YEAR

SOCIAL QUESTIONS

Origins and development.
The employer and the employee.
Employers' societies.
Unions and other employees' societies.
The value and appraisal of professional work in society.
Social institutions.
The individual's own responsibility for himself. State aid.

PROTECTION OF THE INDIVIDUAL BY THE LAW

The basis of law.
The basic rights of man.
The protection of property, the preservation and handing down of property.
Penal law. Punishable actions, the meaning and purpose of punishment, means of and infliction of punishment, ages for subjection to punishment.
Law regarding punishment of young people.
Procedure in ordinary and special courts.

THE GREATER POLITICAL COMMUNITIES

The participation of the people in the life of the State.
Political parties as agencies for forming the opinion of the people.
The 'Land'[3] of Baden-Württemberg: population and territory.
The 'Land' constitution as a basis for citizenship of the Federal Republic, the function of the 'Land' parliament with regard to legislation, the government and administration of the 'Land', the tasks of the 'Land', the 'Land' finances.

Germany as a whole: the Federal Republic as a federation of the West German states, the Basic Constitution as the basis of the union, symbols of the State, the formation and tasks of the Federal organs, the Federal finances, Berlin, the central corridor and East Germany.
Democracy as a way of life.
The rules of democracy.
Humanity, tolerance, and moral courage.

THE STATE AS A POWER REPRESENTING ORDER

Order is assured by the State: the necessary ways of enforcing order.
The power of the people and of the State.

The citizens of the State and the territory of the State.
Forms of State and government.
The limits to the power of the State.
Distribution of the powers, the characteristics of the constitutional State.
Current events, commemoration days and revision.

THIRD YEAR

FROM THE FIRST WORLD WAR TO THE PRESENT DAY

Causes and course of the First World War.
The world powers at the end of the First World War.
The peace treaty and the League of Nations.
The Weimar Republic: foreign and home policy, the world economic crisis.
The road to the totalitarian state.
The domination of the national socialists by force and German resistance.
Foreign policy and the course to the catastrophe of the Second World War.

GERMANY IN THE COMMUNITY OF RACES

The political philosophies of the West and of the East.
Organizations which exist between the Western Powers on the political, economic and cultural levels. Striving for European unity.
The Eastern bloc and world communism.
Non-bloc states.
Aid to underdeveloped countries.
Current topics, remembrance days, and revision.[4]

For our part, we are left to judge the value of the German civics lessons according to the aims and syllabuses which are laid out in the educational directives. From this standpoint and from the knowledge and attitude of today's young Germans, it is obvious that the teaching of civics is of great value in bringing the youngster to think of the meaning of the State and to develop a feeling of his own responsibility for it. Unfortunately, the post-war heritage of a divided Germany, while it can be used to point the moral that neighbouring countries, having three times in seventy years suffered cruelty as a result of German nationalism and expansionist aims, end by dividing Germany in the attempt to prevent another such holocaust, can also be used to stir vengeful emotion and willingness for self-sacrifice in the cause of a united Germany. One visitor to German vocational schools has reported that in five or six such schools he found the civics lessons were little more than propaganda, not merely for reuniting East Germany and West Germany but also for bringing into an enlarged German State parts of what are now Poland and Czechoslovakia. Such educational philosophies have also been found in vocational schools for girls as well as in those for boys: 'We teach our girls to be prepared to die like men,' said one Headmistress, when she was reproached by the English visitor, regarding the nationalism he had found in the civics lesson.

The vocational schools are now largely in new, modern buildings housing workshop, laboratory, and kitchen equipment of the latest design, and are pulsating with fresh, invigorating energy, pointing to the continued success of Germany's economy. The number of hours' attendance at vocational school varies from Land to Land and this depends also on the trade in which the youngster is employed. In fact, the majority of young people in the Federal Republic attend vocational school for between six and eight hours per week, for forty weeks in the year. They attend either for two half-days each week or for one full day, the latter being the more suitable arrangement. A small percentage of the young people at vocational school attend for twelve or more hours in the week and it is hoped that eventually all German youngsters will be able to attend for twelve or even sixteen hours in the week.

In order to ensure that the vocational schools are in fact imparting up-to-date knowledge and methods, there exists a committee whose task it is to see that the schools are working in the closest co-operation with, and for the greatest benefit of, both trade and industry. This committee is made up of the mayor, representatives from trade and industry (both employers and employees), representatives of the teaching staff of the school, and representatives of the parents' association. It acts in a consultative capacity with regard to matters concerning curricula, workshop equipment, and school organization.

Since Kerschensteiner's first six schools were set up, the German vocational school system has shown tremendous expansion and development. The schools all follow the principle that their teaching should be centred on professional training, each school concentrating on certain groups of trades and professions. It could be said that the main spheres of human activity come under four main headings: the home, growing food, producing goods, and trading. Accordingly, there are four main categories of vocational school, each of which concentrates on one of these fields of activity. The domestic vocational schools[5] train girls in the running of a home and family rearing; the agricultural vocational schools[6] train farmers; the industrial and trades vocational schools[7] train workers who work for an increasing output of manufacture, and the commercial vocational schools[8] give training to those who are employed either in selling goods or in administration.

The industrial and trades vocational schools have the longest tradition, and will be treated first in the following survey of the German vocational schools.

THE INDUSTRIAL AND TRADES VOCATIONAL SCHOOLS

The teaching in these schools, as in all the other vocational schools, is centred on the various trades in which the students are employed: the trades which are taught in these schools naturally fall into several main categories, such as trades in the metal industry, in the electrical industry, in the clothing industry and graphic trade, in the building industry, foods, and health service. Then, apart from these trades which fall into clearly definable groups, the schools also cater for young people who are employed as hairdressers, photographers, garage attendants, or for those who are in other varying professions.

Despite the large number of trades for which the industrial and trades vocational schools[9] cater, the observer is at once impressed by the enormous amount of detailed organization in them which gives them their extreme efficiency. For every trade there are well-qualified teachers available, who have received special training for vocational school teaching in one of the Institutes of Technical Education. The admirable new schools built since the last war also offer excellent facilities for practical work, to which about one-quarter of all the teaching time is usually devoted.

Hundreds of students pass through the doors of just one of these schools each week, and the vast majority of them are fortunate enough to walk into classes which give specialized teaching in their own particular trade. To take an example: there may be specialized classes for anything up to thirty different trades in the metal industry – classes for locksmiths, goldsmiths, bodywork builders, lorry mechanics, tool-makers, central heating manufacturers, etc. For students employed in the clothing industry specialized classes may be offered in the different branches of the work, such as the tailoring of ladies' coats, ladies' clothes in general, men's suits and coats, men's underwear, furs, millinery, underwear, and shoemaking.

Sometimes the individual industrial and trades vocational schools cannot do full justice to the large scope which a particular industry offers, such as, for instance, the building industry. In cases like these, a special school is usually set up, which centres all its teaching around the particular industry concerned, such as the catering trade or the building industry, as aforementioned. These specialized vocational schools are usually only to be found in the large towns.

Whatever the student's trade, there are always facilities for his vocational education in Germany. Even if he intends to take up a less-frequently practised trade, such as being a chimney-sweep, or an organ builder or a brewer, the youngster is still bound by law to receive proper professional training and to attend a recognized establishment for that purpose. If he is employed in some such unusual or highly specialized trade, where it is probable that the local industrial and trades vocational school either has no facilities or inadequate ones for giving proper instruction in the necessary subjects, then the student must attend a full-time eight-week course at a suitable regional school. The regional vocational school, like the specialized school mentioned above, gives specialized instruction in one particular field and, because its students may live many miles away, residential accommodation at the school may be provided. Youngsters who are obliged to attend the regional vocational school, because of lack of facilities for instruction in their own trade at the ordinary part-time vocational school, are young people employed as piano- and violin-makers, dental assistants and dental technicians, television mechanics, dairymen, potters, cement workers, brewers, and chemical dry cleaners – to quote just a few of the many and varied occupations whose training is catered for in these specialized regional schools.

The reader will remember that Kerschensteiner's principle was to base the whole of the teaching of the vocational schools on the students' trade, and, from that basis, so to broaden the scope of the teaching that the students eventually gained an insight and understanding into the changing yet changeless pattern of the world, where every force and every person interacted, the one on the other, in the formation of that

The Modern German Vocational Schools · 95

unified harmony which is life. The students were to realize that all the citizens in the State were interdependent, that without the farmer they could not eat, that without the builder they would be homeless, that without steady production, increased trade, and a balanced economy the State could not prosper. They were to be made conscious of the fact that they all shared the responsibility for the continuous advancement and welfare of the State.

Kerschensteiner's theories have had considerable influence on the organization of the modern vocational schools, which, as has been shown, are characterized by similar aims, namely, on the one hand, to give the student an insight and understanding into the organic and spiritual order in world forces, and on the other, to educate him to be a useful and morally conscious individual in the community. The modern Germans, too, see the path to the realization of these aims as lying in trade education. Here the student is not merely given practical and theoretical instruction in the skills of his own particular trade but he also learns to understand the importance and significance of his trade in relation to others, which are closely connected to his own. He learns to assess the position of his own trade within the broader framework of the whole industry and to recognize its dependence on other trades, in the same way as others are dependent on his own. For instance, a bricklayer is not just taught how to lay bricks but is shown all the other stages in the building of a house, so that he can see the importance of his trade and its relationship to the other trades in the industry. At the end of his vocational school training he will be familiar with the various processes involved in the actual manufacture of the bricks, the different stages in building, the historical development of the building trade, the part played by the employers, employees, and the unions. He will see his trade as being a constituent part of the whole industry, which in turn effects the economy of the nation, and he will see himself as a link in that organism. This teaching is given in the lessons in trade instruction, and, in its broader aspects, in the civics lessons which have already been outlined.

It has been mentioned before that the number of teaching periods per week varies in different regions of West Germany, and in some cases local circumstances force the number of hours of instruction to be lower than the authorities would desire. In fact, the majority of the 72,000 classes in the West German vocational schools have between six and eight hours of instruction per week. Rather less than 10,000 classes enjoy more than eight hours per week and, at the other end of the scale, roughly the same number have five or even fewer hours.

The structure of the curriculum, too, varies slightly in different states of the Federal Republic. For instance, it will be seen from the two timetables quoted below that Baden-Württemberg in the South, where the first Sunday schools originated, still retains religious instruction as a subject in its vocational schools. On the other hand, the city-state of Bremen, an industrial protestant city in the North, which has no tradition of religious instruction in its vocational schools, does not incorporate it into its teaching, but does include physical training. The timetables on page 97 are both of industrial and trades schools and, although they are intended for students employed in completely different types of trades, the common factors in the organization of the curriculum emerge quite clearly. At the centre of the teaching stands trade instruction with all its various and varying aspects. This is complemented by instruction in general subjects, of which an essential one is the study and application of the German language.

The teachers in the industrial and trades vocational schools are usually required to be graduates of the technical university or of an institution of higher technical education and must have had a specified amount of practical experience in industry before entering upon teacher training in one of the special Institutes or Universities for Technical Education. These are to be found in Dortmund, Frankfurt, Hamburg, Hannover, Munich, Saarbrücken, Stuttgart, and Wilhelmshaven. Other training departments are being established in more universities. The training course for these vocational school teachers usually lasts two to three years.

The instructors in practical work, which has had a place in vocational education since Kerschensteiner's work in Munich, are drafted in from the various trades and industries, so that the pupils are able to receive their instruction from teachers who are fully conversant with modern methods and procedure. In order that the teachers remain abreast of new trends and developments they meet at regular intervals and form study groups, where they receive further instruction and discuss different aspects of their work.

FOR THOSE EMPLOYED IN THE HAIRDRESSING TRADE (Bremen)

	hours per week
Civics	$\frac{1}{2}$
The State, the law, and economics	$1\frac{1}{2}$
Correspondence	$\frac{1}{2}$
German	$\frac{1}{2}$
Trade instruction	2
Trade arithmetic	$\frac{1}{2}$
Trade drawing	1
Applied trade instruction	$1\frac{1}{2}$
Physical training	1
Total hours	9

FOR MECHANICS (Baden-Württemberg)

	1st yr	2nd yr	3rd yr
Religious instruction	1	1	1
Civics	1	1	1
German	1	1	1
Economics	1	1	1
Trade instruction	2	2	$2\frac{1}{2}$
Trade arithmetic	1	1	$1\frac{1}{2}$
Applied geometry	1	1	–
Trade drawing	2	2	2
Total hours	10	10	10
Practical work	2	2	2

THE COMMERCIAL VOCATIONAL SCHOOLS

Schools which offer commercial training are particularly important, for in Germany there are twice as many apprentices in commerce as there are in industry (500,000 in commerce and 250,000 in industry). There is often a certain amount of overlapping of trades taught in both the industrial and trades schools and in the commercial vocational schools, especially in the country districts. In communities with a low population the young people engaged in commerce may receive their vocational training in the commercial section of the local industrial and trades vocational school. Conversely, the city girl may have a choice of several commercial schools which she may attend. In addition to the ordinary general commercial vocational schools there also exist commercial vocational schools which may specialize in any particular branch of trade or commerce for which there is a high demand. For instance, the working girl in Bremen who is employed in some field of commerce has a choice of six commercial vocational schools. Two of the schools are of the more general type and cater for various aspects of the trade; one concentrates on the catering trade (and provides specialized classes for trades as varied as hotel waitressing, butchery, confectionery, brewers and distillers, cooks); another school specializes in the retail trade and offers specialized classes for shop assistants in all types of wares from foodstuffs to glassware, books, cameras, and leatherware; another school specializes in the wholesale and export trades; and the last school trains employees of bank and insurance companies, and so on. From this brief survey of just one town, it can be seen that the young German girl engaged in trade or commerce has facilities for her professional training equal to those of her male counterpart who is employed in industry.

Like the teaching in the industrial and trades vocational schools, the teaching in the commercial vocational schools, too, is centred on trade instruction, and specialized classes are set up wherever possible. The schools deal with youngsters who are employed in many different activities: there are those employed in some kind of office work, either in public administration or in private concerns; Post Office workers; doctors', opticians', and dentists' assistants; shop assistants and window dressers. The curriculum shows a similar balance between trade subjects and general subjects as in the industrial and trades schools, and all the vocational schools are characterized by similar aims of citizenship education.

The achievements of the industrial and trades, and commercial vocational schools are apparent in many spheres of human activity: the industrial trainees put their well-trained efforts into efficient production for the State economy, and the commercial students are engaged in administration and trade. On the day-to-day level, it is perhaps the German housewife who obtains the most personal contact with the commercial vocational school students, for every shop assistant from whom she buys her wares has had a vocational school training and knows *how* to sell her goods. The German shop assistants are efficient, helpful, and courteous (they would never dream of serving their customers without having politely greeted them first). As a result of their training they have a sound knowledge of the wares which they are selling, of the raw materials from which they are manufactured, of the methods of manufacture, storage, and so on, and are able to advise the customer which product will suit his particular requirements and circumstances. It becomes evident to the customer that the assistant is in full command of his work and so he has complete confidence in the assistant's advice and recommendations. In this way, shopkeepers and assistants occupy a privileged position in the community, for they have the power to influence the taste and standards of the consumer public. They themselves have a fairly detailed knowledge of the wares they are selling, and can guide and train the customer to distinguish between materials of good and bad quality, between design of good and poor taste. And so, in the long run, the influence of the vocational school extends much farther than just to its own students, but reaches out to embrace the ranks of the general public.

The majority of German apprentices attend either the industrial and trades vocational school or the commercial vocational school, when they leave full-time schooling and go out to work. Here, it must be remembered that in Germany the term 'apprentice' may be applied to much more extensive a group of youngsters than in England.[10] The German youngster is indentured as an apprentice in many occupations for which no formal apprenticeship is served in England. For instance, youngsters employed as shop assistants or clerks all serve an apprenticeship in Germany, and, in their capacity as apprentices, do not reap the financial gains which the working teenager in England enjoys. Instead, they receive only a token payment.

Those who are not employed in what is classified as 'skilled work', and who therefore do not serve an apprenticeship, are, nevertheless, still required by German law to receive a part-time education. Boys who come into this category, i.e. those employed in semi-skilled or unskilled occupations, are usually drafted into the industrial and trades vocational schools, where they are encouraged to think more in terms of obtaining some kind of skilled work: in Germany there is no maximum age limit for entering into an apprenticeship. The girls in unskilled work usually attend the domestic vocational schools.

THE DOMESTIC VOCATIONAL SCHOOLS

The domestic vocational schools cater for the education of those girls who have taken up 'conveyor-belt' or other unskilled work, in addition to that of girls who are employed in some kind of domestic service. Since many of the girls in attendance at this type of school follow no trade which requires skills or training, the principle that trade instruction should form the basis of the teaching cannot really be put into practice here. Because of this lack of a common skilled trade, the schools therefore seize the one interest which is shared by all the girls – the interest in marriage and family life – and endeavour to set this aspect of human life at the centre of their teaching. The interest in marriage is usually strong among these girls: they show little interest in their occupation as such, which, for the most part, they regard as being merely a stop-gap until the time when they become married and rear a family.

The domestic vocational schools have aims similar to those of the other types of vocational schools and feel, too, that they have a particular role to play in helping their students to adapt themselves to their new way of life as workers. For the girls who attend the domestic vocational schools are often of a lower intelligence and come from the lower social strata, and it is probable that of all the different types and groups of girls passing from school to adult working life, it is these girls who are likely to find the change-over most difficult.

The teaching in the schools aims at developing in the student the practical skills required of a wife and mother and also gives her theoretical knowledge pertaining to home-running. At the same time, the domestic vocational school training is placed on as wide a base as possible, so that she is not restricted purely to the acquisition of skills and knowledge connected with motherhood but has also a general interest in the broader aspects of life. She is encouraged to take an active interest in the further development of her own personality and talents, and when she leaves the vocational school she will have been made familiar with women's organizations and societies which she could join whereby she could remain in contact with other people and new ideas and develop her social talents.

The subjects in the curriculum at the domestic vocational school fall naturally into three groups: firstly, there are social and general subjects such as civics, the home and family, German, household accounts and correspondence. The second group is comprised of subjects connected with the care and rearing of children, such as the care of the sick and the healthy, baby-care and child-rearing and dietetics. The third group is made up of practical subjects, for which both a practical and theoretical training is given, such as cookery and nutrition, needlework and materials, housework, including washing and ironing, and gardening. It can be seen that the broad lines of the curriculum ensure that the girls obtain a sure and comprehensive grounding for their later status in life.

Kerschensteiner had always stressed the importance of the home and environment for the development of children,[11] who, after all, spend more time at home than they do at school. This is one aspect of education which is receiving an increasing amount of attention in Germany, with respect to vocational school education. The Germans realize the significance of the role which the vocational schools could play in giving this essential training in motherhood and home-management and there are hopes that some kind of instruction in the arts of home-making will eventually be introduced into the commercial vocational school too, where it would be an obligatory subject, studied in addition to the normal curriculum in the present commercial vocational school. Another possibility for ensuring that a greater percentage of German girls have this type of instruction would be to extend the scope of the domestic science teaching within the system of basic full-time education. At the present time, domestic science teaching is not even incorporated into the curriculum of the German Gymnasien and receives but little attention in the elementary schools.

Domestic science instruction, such as is given in the domestic vocational schools has already been given an important place in the curriculum of Baden-Württemberg's vocational schools for rural and domestic studies. These schools, which cater for the rural female population, exist as yet only in Baden-Württemberg, where there are some four hundred of them. The organization of this type of school is very similar to that of the domestic vocational school, but, as the name suggests, it also offers instruction which is of particular relevance to the everyday life and conditions of the rural youth. These schools, which have sprung up since the last war, show themselves to be the direct equivalent of Kerschensteiner's own rural continuation schools for girls, adapted, naturally, to the requirements of modern times. They do not place as much emphasis as did Kerschensteiner's schools on gardening and agriculture, but in their very conception and principles prove themselves to be the fruit of the seeds which Kerschensteiner sowed.

AGRICULTURAL VOCATIONAL SCHOOLS

The last main branch in the German vocational school system is the agricultural vocational school, which also owes its existence, to a large extent, to the pioneering work of Kerschensteiner. Although Kerschensteiner had drawn the attention of German educationists to the lack of facilities for the professional training of farmers, this branch of vocational training remained largely overlooked until the economic crises of the 1920s forced a reappraisal of the situation. In the late 1920s and early 1930s a serious start was finally made at tackling the problem.

The schools follow the same principles as Kerschensteiner had intended, and there are now some four hundred and fifty of them in West Germany; they are attended by about 5 per cent of the total vocational school population. The curriculum shows the same balance of trade and general subjects as is apparent in other types of German vocational schools. The trade instruction covers such fields as animal care, cultivation of cereals, forage, soils and manures, fruit, wines and trees, agricultural machines and implements, and agricultural arithmetic. Opportunity is also given for practical work.

CONCLUSION

Thus all German youngsters who are not engaged in full-time education are obliged to attend a vocational school, where they study on a part-time basis until the age of eighteen or until the termination of their apprenticeship, thus continuing their link with education. It is unfortunate that sometimes vocational school attendance comes in addition to a full working week, which means, in effect, that the youngsters are working for five days and attending school on the sixth. This is obviously a very great disadvantage in the system, and it is hoped that any such scheme of vocational schooling adopted in

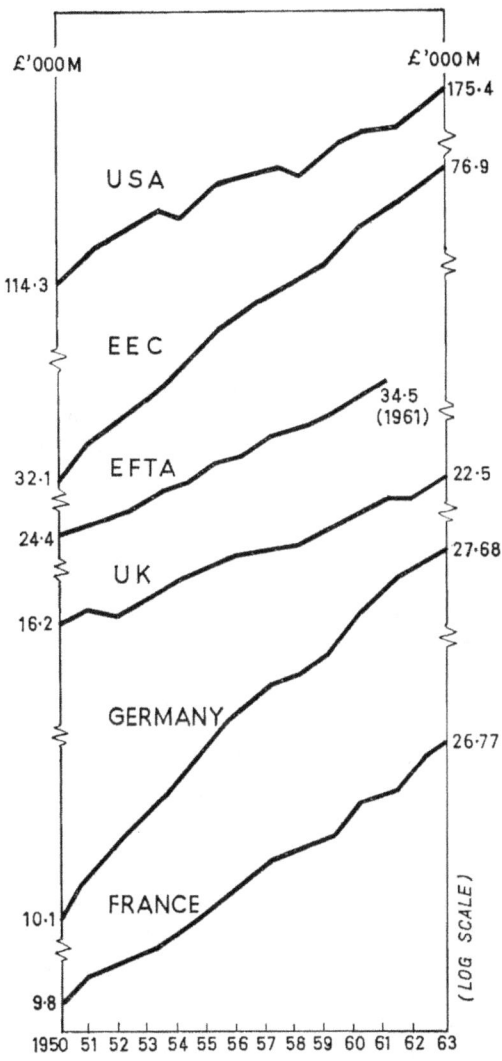

GROSS NATIONAL PRODUCT 1950–63
from a table published in *The Times*, 29 September, 1964
The figures are based on constant 1954 prices

this country would ensure that school attendance be counted as part of the working week and not as being in addition to it. Yet, whatever the structural defects of the German system, it does achieve its aim of ensuring that absolutely all young people continue their links with education at least up to the age of eighteen.

Although the vocational schools do not set up examinations themselves, the apprenticeship is terminated by an examination which is run under the auspices of the Chamber of Industry and Commerce or the Chamber of Handicrafts, which play a large part in the organization and inspection of apprenticeship training. The examination is practical, written, and oral, and the work which the student has performed at vocational school is taken into account. If the examination is passed, the worker, if he is employed in industry, obtains the skilled worker's certificate; if he is employed in the handicrafts, he obtains the journeyman's certificate. When he has gained these certificates the worker automatically goes on to a higher rate of pay.

The vocational schools, along with all the other types of schools in Germany, are suffering from a shortage of teachers, but all those who are engaged in vocational school teaching are well qualified for their work, having undertaken special training for vocational school teaching.

The vocational schools are now a permanent feature of everyday life in Germany, as vital a branch of education as are the full-time basic schools. They play an important part educationally, and in addition to this they also contribute to the training of Germany's skilled manpower, on whom Germany, to a large extent, bases her economy. Her efficient and planned training schemes and vocational school system have combined to help achieve an increase in production far greater than that achieved in this country.

In an age of growing specialization it is essential that we train our workers effectively. At the same time, it is equally important that we should follow Germany's example and pay attention not only to the brighter boys who take up apprenticeships but that we should concentrate also on improving the education and training of the duller, Newsom youngsters, many of whom in future years would otherwise constitute an 'unemployable rump'.[12]

8 · Further Technical Education in Modern Germany

KERSCHENSTEINER'S VOLUNTARY CLASSES

An examination of the system of military service lay beyond Kerschensteiner's sphere of activities, but his influence with regard to an effective system of continued education for skilled workers, journeymen, and 'masters' laid a solid and permanent basis for the very good work now being achieved in that field in Germany today. Kerschensteiner recognized that all true education inspired the educand with a desire for increased knowledge and skills, and stressed that his desire to learn must always be furthered and fulfilled. He insisted that the opportunity for self-betterment and an increase in knowledge must be made available to people from all walks of life, whatever their age or status.

With this end in view, Kerschensteiner vigorously set in motion a scheme for the introduction of voluntary classes at the continuation schools, designed to be attended by workers who had already completed their apprenticeship and who were desirous of further vocational or general education. The principles governing the choice of subjects in the curriculum corresponded to those which had played a dominant part in his organization of the ordinary part-time continuation schools, namely, that professional education was to be the root from which all general and civic education should grow. Even the theme of the so-called 'general course' was based on the worker's environment; subjects of instruction included such topics as economic history, history of handicrafts, commercial geography, hygiene, trade instruction, and insurance law and constitutional law.

Specialized classes which gave instruction to members of a specific trade were soon opened for journeymen in many different trades and immediately gained immense popularity. They, too, were connected with a relevant trade society and enjoyed benefits similar to those which the ordinary continuation schools had as a result of their connexion with trade associations. Instruction took place in the evenings and on Sundays, and a minimum number of five hours' instruction per week was imposed. In addition to these courses, Kerschensteiner also initiated other courses which demanded attendance for between thirty and forty-eight hours per week. The huge success of all these various courses for adult workers is shown by the attendance figures: in 1908 there were already 1,500 students, and by 1912 this figure had more than doubled and the number of applicants far surpassed the number of places available.

Alongside Kerschensteiner's new voluntary courses for journeymen and 'masters' there already existed other types of trade schools and technical schools. Out of all these various types of schools and courses has evolved Germany's vigorous system of further technical education, which has produced the skilled specialists for whom Germany is celebrated. A complex system of full-time courses in technical and higher technical schools has developed, which give all levels of training up to the higher executive grade, and from which students may, if they wish, and if they are of suitable calibre, pass into the technical university. Whatever the profession of the student, whatever grade or standard he has attained in that profession, there are always facilities for further training open to the German worker,[1] whereby he may pursue his vocational knowledge and improve his qualifications and personal efficiency.

PRE-OCCUPATIONAL TRAINING

In addition to the notable work which Kerschensteiner achieved in the sphere of post-apprenticeship training, it must also be borne in mind that, early on in his career in administration, he had already introduced the teaching of handicraft into the elementary schools, thereby creating what might be considered as a form of pre-occupational, preparatory training.

Within the framework of the modern system of basic schooling in Germany, pre-occupational training seems to have attracted little attention up till now, although at least some of the states intend to review this question, or have already done so.[2] Normally, pre-occupational training is catered for in the period following the completion of normal compulsory, full-time schooling. In recent years a new type of school has come into existence, whose sole purpose it is to give pre-occupational instruction. These schools are attended by youngsters who have completed their compulsory full-time schooling but who have not yet taken up their chosen occupation.

At the present time the pre-occupational schools[3] are attended only by a low percentage of the total number of students engaged in vocational and technical education. From this it is to be deduced that the vast majority of West German school-leavers prefer to take up an apprenticeship straight away, rather than enter upon a full-time course at a pre-occupational school, lasting one, two, or sometimes even three years, before starting work. The student who does decide to undertake a course of study at some kind of non-compulsory vocational school, such as this type, is then automatically freed from the obligation to attend the normal part-time vocational school, provided a certain minimum number of hours attendance has been completed at the full-time school.

These pre-occupational schools, of which many are private, offer courses which give training in a variety of trades and professions, and, in all of them, the hours of instruction vary between thirty and thirty-six per week. At the moment, there are twice as many girls attending pre-occupational school as boys, for a large percentage of them cater for the predominantly female professions, such as administrative work, domestic service, catering, commerce, and work with children. The industrial trades are scarcely represented. When finally taking up employment, the student from the pre-occupational school finds himself in a favoured position on the labour market, for the employers prefer to take on youngsters who already have a good grounding in the theoretical and practical sides of the work and who do not need to be released from their employment to attend the part-time vocational school. The other advantage of the pre-occupational school student over the normal apprentice is that his knowledge, which has been gained through more concentrated study in a shorter time, is likely to be on a more solid basis and of a more permanent nature than that of the ordinary apprentice, who had to wait for a week between each set of lessons.

However, this does mean that after his one or two years of continued education, the pre-occupational school student is then completely cut off from any further educational influences (apart, of course, from those to which he voluntarily submits himself), whereas, the youngster who goes out to a working life straight away, remains under the influence and guidance of the vocational school at least until the age of eighteen. He is therefore likely to derive a greater educational and moral benefit from this prolonged period of teaching, which he receives at a stage in his life when he is having to make considerable adjustments both as a worker, and also with regard to his spiritual and emotional development. Also, by the time he leaves vocational school he is approaching a certain level of insight and maturity, which enable him to gain a truer appreciation of the real value of the education, which he has, up till that time, only accepted through habit.

TECHNICAL SCHOOLS [4]

Kerschensteiner's introduction of the voluntary evening classes for journeymen marked the starting-point for the rapid growth of a complex system of technical college courses which enable the German worker to continue his professional training, either in part-time or full-time study.

As has been shown in the previous chapter, the large majority of the elementary and middle school pupils in Germany go straight out to work at the end of their compulsory schooling. They then attend the ordinary vocational school on one day a week for roughly three years, during their apprenticeship training. At the end of this period they obtain their certificate as 'journeyman' if they are employed in handicrafts, or as 'skilled worker' if they are employed in industry. The worker who wishes to pursue his training beyond this level must then work for a minimum of five years practising his trade, before he is allowed to sit the examination which gives him the qualification of 'master'. As a 'master' he is then allowed to take in and train his own apprentices in his own business. Alternatively, if he is employed in an industrial concern, he can then take up some more responsible position, where he is employed in a supervisory capacity. Before he sits this examination, the would-be 'master' must take a course of preparation at a technical school.

These technical schools play a significant role in the vocational school system, for they are of considerable value in the systematic, further education of the German adult population. The courses which are offered in the schools are varied, in subject, in level of achievement and in duration, and may be followed either on a full-time or a part-time (evening) basis. Candidates for the 'master' examination, for instance, usually attend either a full-time course lasting one year, or, alternatively, attend evening courses which are spread out over a longer period of time. The subjects of study at the technical schools are centred on the various trades, but at the same time instruction in general, cultural subjects is also given.

Since the last war, especially, more attention is being paid in Germany to training in the human aspects of the work which the students at the technical schools will undertake when they have completed their studies. The majority of the students will be employed later in some kind of supervisory capacity, where the maintenance of good personal relations with employees is a contributory factor in all successful and happy work. To meet this very real side of working life, many technical schools have now introduced into their curricula for future 'masters' lessons in leadership, character judgement, and human relations. For if the spirit in the firm is to be one of co-operation and respect, the 'masters' and foremen must not only be efficient workers themselves, but must possess vigorous personalities and an understanding of simple human relations. They must be in a position to understand the problems and difficulties of the men who are working under them, if they are to encourage a healthy working atmosphere, where the workers take pride in their work and are keen for the success of the enterprise.

The technical schools are often housed in the same buildings as the ordinary vocational schools, and, whereas Kerschensteiner's initial voluntary evening classes for journeymen offered training in only a limited number of trades, the modern German technical schools cater for trades and professions as far apart as brewers, bakers, photographers, interior decorators, joiners, lorry mechanics, and bookbinders. In the technical age, where production methods are rapidly changing, the technical schools are carrying out an important function in their attempts to keep their adult students abreast of modern trends and developments in their own particular trade.

TECHNICIAN SCHOOLS [5]

In recent years, similar schools have also come into existence, connected mostly with the various branches of the metal and electronic trades, for the purpose of training technicians in industry.

On entering the schools, the students may either take a one-year, full-time course or a part-time evening course lasting three years. Both of these programmes of study are terminated by an examination, the successful completion of which gives the student the qualification of 'State-examined firm technician'. The training offered in these schools gives the students a more detailed and specialized technical knowledge than the 'masters' in industry receive at the technical school. Successful students go on to occupy the middle posts in industry, where they are employed as skilled technicians.

HIGHER TECHNICAL SCHOOLS [6]

The technical and technician schools play a vital part in the German scheme of professional training, for they ensure that Germany is furnished with a regular supply of skilled and responsible operatives in trade and industry. With equal care and thoroughness, the Germans have also organized a system of higher technical schools which cater for the training of the higher personnel in industry. The higher technical schools and engineering schools are attended by students who wish to take up posts which require a higher level of specialized knowledge than that which is offered at the ordinary technical school and yet which do not demand a university education: such posts may be those of sector or departmental managers or even works' managers.

Candidates who apply for entry into these schools are required to have had two or three years' practical experience in industry and to have obtained either the certificate of maturity from the middle school or the certificate of maturity for entrance into a technical school. This latter certificate is gained after successful completion of special extension courses organized and pursued at the ordinary part-time vocational school. The higher technical schools are regional schools and give specialized training in one particular trade or industry, offering courses of three years' duration, terminated by an examination. Despite the natural emphasis on all aspects of professional training, the higher technical schools also provide general instruction, which is a characteristic of the entire vocational and technical school system in Germany.

The engineering schools[7] fall into the same category as the higher technical schools and are governed by similar entrance requirements. The students who obtain good marks in their final examinations at the engineering school also have a further field of study open to them, for they may gain entry to the technical university, an institution which is of long standing in Germany, and whose course lasts a minimum of four years. Here the students may find themselves studying alongside ex-Gymnasium pupils, who, having obtained the Abitur, the university matriculation certificate, have then spent some six to twelve months in industry before proceeding to study at the technical university. When they successfully terminate their studies, the students gain the most coveted prize of all engineers – the Diploma in Engineering, a qualification which is roughly equivalent to our M.Sc.Engg.

In the race for the higher positions in German industry there often exists competition between the engineers who have received their training at the Gymnasium and technical university, and those who have had the more practically biased training offered by the extension classes at the vocational school and who have then gone on to engineering school. There is often a tendency for the university-trained engineer to look down on his technical school-trained colleague in Germany, where pure academic qualifications have always been held in high esteem. (The emphasis on and respect for paper qualifications is illustrated by the way in which, in correspondence with a German who has a title, the title *precedes* the name: the proud possessor of the Diploma in Engineering for example, is not Herr Schmidt, Dip.-Ing., but instead, Dip.-Ing. Herr Schmidt.)

FURTHER TRAINING IN COMMERCE

Further education in trade and industry bears a longer tradition than does that offered to employees in commerce. However, despite the initial lead which was shown in the introduction of industrial and trades courses, the distribution of man-power has changed so considerably in Germany today that there are twice as many apprentices in commerce as there are in industry. (The number of commercial apprentices has increased fourfold since 1947.) Thus commercial training assumes a greater significance and is catered for in a similar system of further education to that which is enjoyed by industrial apprentices in Germany.

COMMERCIAL PRE-OCCUPATIONAL SCHOOLS [8]

Out of all the pre-occupational schools in the Federal Republic the largest number of any one single type is that of the commercial pre-occupational schools. These schools saw their beginnings in the 1920s when they offered courses of training in the new and necessary arts of shorthand and typing. Now there are over eight hundred of these schools.

These commercial or business schools mostly give full-time courses lasting two years and are attended mainly by girls. The schools bear the same characteristics as do the vocational schools and other types of pre-occupational schools, namely, that in addition to increasing the professional skills of their students, they also aim at an improvement in the standard of their general education. For instance, girls who will later take up posts in commerce or administration are likely to study the following subjects at commercial school: German, history, religious instruction, commercial arithmetic, English, commercial economics and correspondence, office work, shorthand, typing, bookkeeping, gymnastics, and housekeeping.

HIGHER COMMERCIAL SCHOOLS [9]

The commercial pre-occupational schools are attended by girls who come directly from the elementary school and who desire a basic training in the skills of their trade as well as a continued general education, so that they may then find employment in some branch of business. The girls who already possess a higher level of basic education, such as those who have attended the middle school or the Gymnasium, have the opportunity of attending the higher commercial school, which gives a more advanced training than does the ordinary commercial pre-occupational school. Former elementary school pupils who prove themselves to be of the necessary calibre also have the possibility of entering the higher commercial school, provided that first of all they undertake a preparatory course lasting one year.

Unlike the higher technical school and engineering school, the higher commercial school is entirely pre-occupational. That is to say, whereas the higher technical schools require their students to have

Further Technical Education in Modern Germany · 113

undergone a specific amount of practical experience in their trade before embarking on their further studies, the higher commercial school is attended by students who have come directly from their basic full-time schooling.

The course of instruction in the higher commercial schools lasts from two to three years, with an average of thirty-three lessons per week. Like the ordinary commercial pre-occupational schools, these schools give both a vocational and general education.

THE ECONOMICS HIGH SCHOOL[10]

Another form of higher technical school is the economics high school, which was introduced in the years immediately preceding the Second World War. As the name suggests, this school is concerned with imparting an education which stresses the economic subjects, such as economic history, economic geography, industrial economy. This school is rather different in its constitution and organization from the other types of higher schools which have so far received consideration here, for, whereas all the other higher technical schools have as their first task the training for a profession, the economics high school also prepares its students for the university matriculation certificate, the Abitur. While it definitely does devote more time in its programme to the economic subjects, its basic aim, however, is not to produce specialists in economics, but to educate its students to be thinking responsible citizens.

The length of the course leading to the Abitur is of three years' duration. Some German states, however, do not rank the economics high school as a full secondary school and consequently, the schools in these states do not offer the Abitur course: in these states the economics high school has as its chief task the training of students in business and economic studies.

In those states such as Baden-Württemberg, where the economics high schools do offer a course leading to the Abitur examination, the students are drawn from two sources: they are either former Gymnasium pupils or students who have received good marks in their examinations at the end of the second year of study at the higher commercial school. When their studies at the economics high school have been successfully terminated and the university matriculation certificate has been obtained, the students are then able to proceed to study economics at university, or, if they fulfil certain conditions, they may go on to study in any faculty of the university.

It has thus been shown that, in Germany, girls, as well as boys, have suitable opportunities for their continued education. Although higher vocational education for girls was introduced later than that for boys and has developed more slowly, it also owes its origins, to a large extent, to the work of Kerschensteiner, who was among the first pioneers of full educational facilities for girls. There even exist technical schools for girls engaged in domestic service, and special courses for those working on the land. In fact, this brief survey of opportunities for further education in Germany would not be complete without a mention of the work being achieved for those employed in domestic service and in agriculture, however low the percentage of the total population this involves.

SCHOOLS FOR HOUSEKEEPING[11]

The schools for housekeeping have developed from the old schools for housekeeping which were set up in the years after 1880. The majority of them offer a course which lasts one year and which is pre-occupational. They are characterized by the same aims as the domestic vocational schools, namely, to give the girls an education which will equip them to carry out efficiently their roles of mother and housekeeper. While it may, with justification, be argued that the students are still too young and immature to gain the maximum benefit from this type of course, the positive educational influence exerted on the students during this year of transition from school to working life cannot but yield fruit. An examination is taken at the end of the year, and this is of particular value to those girls who are to be employed in domestic service or in food planning.

TECHNICAL SCHOOLS FOR WOMEN'S PROFESSIONS[12]

A more advanced training in household economy is given at the technical school for women's professions, which is largely a post-war development in the system of vocational education. This school has taken on varying forms in the different states of Western Germany but, on the whole, they all give a general education and lay the stress on the teaching of domestic subjects. Entrants to these schools must

Further Technical Education in Modern Germany · 115

have completed the course at a middle school, or, alternatively, must have passed through the sixth class of a Gymnasium.

The work which is undertaken in these schools is of especial value to young girls who intend to take up positions such as child nurses or nursery school attendants. Further advanced training courses at the schools, combined with specific periods of practical work both at school and in various undertakings, can lead to the qualification called the 'State examination in household economy'. Armed with this qualification, the student is then in a position to take up a post in any sphere of domestic work. Extension courses have also been established for former elementary school pupils, whereby these girls may also receive training in domestic economy at a higher level, which will enable them to find employment as kitchen supervisors, laundry manageresses, and so on. Some schools also provide a course which is terminated by the 'State examination in needlework'.

The two main branches of technical schools which cater for the further education of women, the schools for commerce and the schools for housekeeping, are now well-established institutions within the framework of the German educational system. All of them have undergone a decisive development since Kerschensteiner's insistence, right from the very beginning, on the vital part which the women of a country and the mothers of future citizens have to play in the welfare of the State. Kerschensteiner's demand for their right to facilities in vocational education equal to those of their menfolk is now an accomplished fact in Germany.

FURTHER EDUCATION IN AGRICULTURE

Education in agriculture was also another sphere where Kerschensteiner endeavoured to create equality of opportunity. Further vocational education was to be made available to *all*, for the progress and advancement of the State was dependent on the work and help of *all* its citizens, whatever their occupation. Kerschensteiner considered that the farmers, in particular, had a task of utmost importance to play in the welfare of their country.

Since Kerschensteiner's reform plans were announced, the Germans have done much to ensure that their agricultural workers are not overlooked in questions concerning their education and vocational training. The agricultural worker attends the part-time vocational school for agriculture, and, should he plan eventually either to run a farm of his own or to become a farm manager, there are also facilities for his further training, which will equip him with the knowledge requisite for the success of the enterprise.

The course of study at the technical schools for agriculture[13] takes place during the winter months only, which makes it possible for the students to be engaged in practical work in the summer, when their help on the farm is required most, while the instructors occupy themselves with administrative and consultative work during the summer. These technical schools are only attended after the full three-year course has been completed at the vocational school for agriculture. Attendance is necessary for all those workers who wish to sit the 'master' examination.

The course lasts only one year, basically, but since the instruction is given in the winter months only, the teaching is spread out over two winters. Instruction is given in a very wide range of subjects and topics pertaining to agriculture and gives the students a sound basic knowledge, so that they will be able to tackle the problems and difficulties which confront the farmer, whether they be of a practical or administrative nature. Some idea of the scope of the teaching can be gained from the timetable opposite, which is valid for Baden-Württemberg. Classes are established for girls, too, at these schools and their curriculum is adjusted to suit their particular needs and requirements in rural life. The girls study a variety of subjects, which form a combination of the domestic subjects which are taught at the domestic vocational schools, and of rural studies. The lessons in rural studies are adapted to suit the requirements of womenfolk, and include such aspects of farm work as poultry-keeping, gardening, livestock raising and feeding. The twofold aspect of the work (domestic and rural studies) ensures that the girls are given a good grounding in the skills and knowledge which will help them to be both good mothers and efficient farmers.

There also exist higher technical schools for agriculture.[14] Gifted students who obtain good marks at their examinations in these schools may proceed, if they wish, to the university for agriculture, or, of course, to an Institute of Technical Education, where they will be trained to be teachers in vocational schools for agriculture.

This survey of further professional education in Germany has, by necessity, been a brief one, yet, despite the obvious restrictions and

FIRST YEAR

	Lessons per week
Agricultural chemistry	4
Crop cultivation	4
Rudiments of cultivation and protection of plants	3
Rudiments of animal rearing	3
Organization and management of a farm, with farm description and book-keeping	4
Agrarian constitution, agricultural policy and markets	1
Applied agricultural methods, including basic physics and practical work	4
Fruit-growing	2–3
Wine cultivation	2–3
Forestry	1–4
Animal health	1
Civics	1
General culture	1
Practical youth work	1
Average	34

SECOND YEAR

	Lessons per week
Cultivation and special protection of plants	5–7
Animal rearing and feeding	5–7
Farm organization and bookkeeping	6–7
Taxes	1
Agricultural constitution, etc.	2
Applied agricultural methods, etc.	3
Fruit growing	2–3
Vine cultivation	2–3
Forestry	1–4
Animal health	1
Civics	1
Average	34

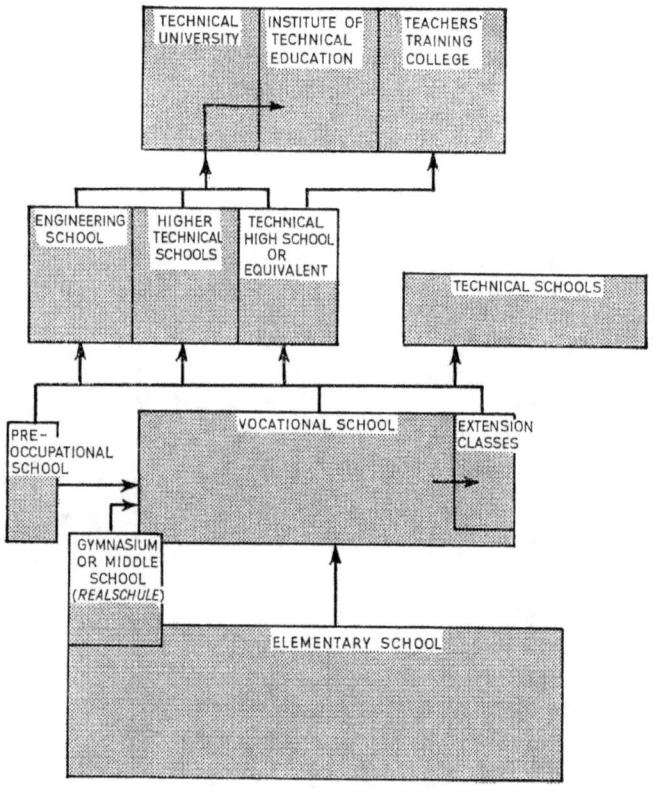

INDUSTRIAL AND TRADE EDUCATION IN GERMANY

Further Technical Education in Modern Germany · 119

limitations which brevity imposes, it is hoped that the reader will have gained some useful impression of the scope of the facilities for further vocational education open to German workers. It is worthy of note that in Germany further professional training is not restricted to workers who are employed in industry, trade, or commerce, which, of course, account for the majority of employees, but that it also embraces agricultural workers and women engaged in domestic employment.

'THE ALTERNATIVE WAY'[15]

One disadvantage of the structure of the German system of further training, however, is its strict rigidity and demand for paper qualifications. Cases, which do arise in England, of an employee starting off his working life on the shop floor and finally achieving a position of great height and esteem in factory management, are scarcely to be found in Germany.

Efforts have been made in recent years to break down the rigid barriers and lines of demarcation which exist between the various branches of education and training in Germany. A system has now been introduced, called the 'alternative way of education', whereby it is made possible for an ex-elementary school pupil to go on to study at university without ever having attended the Gymnasium. According to this system, the student must attend supplementary extension courses at the vocational school, terminated by an examination (Fachschulreife), which accords the maturity certificate requisite for entry into an institution of higher technical education. The student then enters the engineering school, for example, and if he has passed its final examination with the grade 'Good', he is then entitled to a place at technical university. The work of the economic high schools, which may also prepare students for university studies, has already been mentioned.[16] However, despite the opportunities which have been opened by this 'alternative way', there are, in fact, relatively few former elementary school pupils who have the ability or stamina to proceed to university studies.[17]

Despite defects in the system, the scope and opportunity of the facilities for further professional training in Germany must be acknowledged. Whatever his trade and whatever stage or level he has reached in that trade, the German worker has the opportunity to attend courses of further training, whereby he may improve the knowledge and skills needed in his daily work.

By Kerschensteiner's very insistence that voluntary courses for journeymen should be set up, he testified to his conviction that it was not enough to train a person to carry out a particular trade efficiently. The worker must be trained to take pride in achievement, but Kerschensteiner saw that it was of equal importance that the worker's training should educate him to set himself an ever-increasing level of achievement. The hall-mark of true education was that it increased the desire for knowledge and for a higher level of personal perfection and achievement. The modern German system of further professional education, with its complex network of courses, tries to ensure that, for those who have this desire for self-improvement, there exists the opportunity for its fulfilment.

9 · Into the Future

THE LOST OPPORTUNITIES

Despite England's own inability to introduce any scheme of further education as far-reaching as Kerschensteiner's achievements at the beginning of the century, this sad state of affairs is in no way due to a lack of appreciation of Kerschensteiner's work. As early as 1910 an official report, published by H.M.S.O. had stated that: 'Munich may well be proud of what is probably the most perfectly organized and most perfectly equipped system of continuation schools in the world.'[1]

By this time the Munich system of further education was soundly established and in addition to 8 headmasters, 71 teachers were employed full-time and there were 209 elementary school teachers who were employed on a part-time basis. The practical instruction was given by some 188 masters and skilled workers.

A London County Council report published in 1914[2] also showed that the author was very impressed by the German achievements, both regarding the schools themselves and the training of the teachers. These teacher training courses which Kerschensteiner had established lasted one year and were given at regular intervals in Munich. Similar training courses had also been set up in a few towns outside Munich.

In the continuation schools, numbers both of courses and of students increased steadily. As a result both of the implementation of the further education system and of the classes in practical work in the elementary schools, the percentage of skilled workers rose to such an extent that it was estimated that, whereas in London 68 per cent of the working population was engaged in unskilled employment, the figure in Munich was only 10 per cent.[3] The interest in vocational education became no longer confined to Munich, for most of the other German states had by this time realized the national importance of technical education and had introduced trade courses, which, too, were crowned with success. The writer of the L.C.C. report testified to the vigour and energy characteristic of these new schools throughout Germany:

'I was prepared to find unwilling students taking a slovenly interest in their studies, and teachers struggling with the "evils" of forced attendance. Nothing of this kind was seen. Pupils were thoroughly alive to their work, thoroughly interested, and obviously eager to do their best and get the maximum value from their attendance. Teachers were fresh and vigorous and, with no nightmare of disappearing classes, were concentrating their efforts on educational efficiency and getting excellent results. Directors of schools were thorough masters of the situation and were bending their efforts to the best curricula, the best equipment and details of organization in such a way that none of our principals or responsible teachers can possibly do, owing to the multitudinous calls on their time. No money is wasted on advertising, no special system of whipping up large numbers of absentees is required.'[4]

The enthusiasm shown in these two reports testifies to the support in England for Kerschensteiner's reorganized continuation schools. Germany's considerable superiority in the field of vocational education was now well established.

THE COURSE OF TECHNICAL EDUCATION IN ENGLAND

It was the exhibitions of the years 1851 and 1862 which had first aroused Britain to a recognition of the fact that, if her trade were to prosper, she must pay much greater attention to the technical training of her workers. But, it was not until the years from 1870 onwards that any real progress was made regarding the introduction of technical courses. A considerable step forward was undertaken with the foundation of the City and Guilds of London Institute for the Advancement of Technical Education, which held its first examinations in 1880.[5] Two years later appeared the first report of a Royal Commission on technical education. The cause of technical education was then later promoted in a practical way by the funds provided by the 'whisky money' – the tax on whisky. This revenue provided for the establishment of another twenty-five polytechnics and technical institutes, along with more than a hundred science schools, all over the country.

Yet despite the foundations for technical education which were laid during these years, there had evolved, even by the year 1914, no *national* policy or system with regard either to the establishment of schools or to their attendance. There had been no law that technical schools *must* be set up, nor that compulsory attendance should be introduced. The first headway in this matter was not made until the crying need was revealed during the First World War. Hence the clauses of the Fisher Education Act of 1918, which planned the establishment of day continuation schools. These would be attended by all youngsters aged fourteen to eighteen, who were not engaged in full-time education. The principle of day release was to be established, with no lessons taking place after seven in the evening. In January 1921 London opened its first twenty-two day continuation schools,[6] but, in other parts of the country response to the Act was slow: although there were one hundred and forty-five local education authorities concerned with the proposals of the Act, the only authorities which actually succeeded in introducing their schemes (apart from London) were Birmingham, Swindon, Stratford-on-Avon, and Rugby. Of these, only Rugby put through its scheme in its entirety and enforced compulsory attendance.

Some splendid work was achieved in the day continuation schools which had been set up, but, within a year or two of their being established, the majority of them had closed, although some continued to exist as voluntary schools. The proposal to introduce compulsory day continuation schools had been received with hostility by some sections of the popular press, which, in turn, directed public opinion against the schools. Many of the employers, too, were against the scheme, for, according to its conditions, they would be required to release their young workers from their employment for the equivalent of one full working day each week. The actual date for the introduction of the scheme was left open for each individual authority to decide, with the result that employers who were against the schools endeavoured to engage youngsters who resided in an area whose authority had not yet established continuation schools. Other dissenting employers proceeded to engage only those young people whose age was above the upper age limit, as stipulated by the Act, for continuation school attendance. Finally, the whole issue of the continuation schools became a political factor and assumed great importance in the municipal elections. Public opinion was swayed by the popular Press and the educators' hopes for the day continuation schools turned into mere dreams. Some schools continued to exist on a voluntary basis, but in time, their number also diminished.

After the failure to introduce day continuation schools on a wide scale, the general trend of technical education was driven to part-time courses, taken in the evenings, when the students were often already exhausted after a full day's physical work. Despite the difficulties of study, attendance at evening courses steadily increased all over the country, especially after the introduction of National Certificates in 1921, thus showing the willingness on the part of the workers to respond to any opportunity for improving their skill and qualifications.

The economic crises and large-scale unemployment which characterized the intermission years between the wars pointed clearly to the desperate need to set up courses of further education and industrial training. Yet despite the dire urgency of the situation no official action was taken, and the masses of the young employed remained, to a large extent, deprived of the intellectual and physical stimulus which could have been accorded to them by the day continuation schools. It was not until the Butler Education Act, born from the humanitarian idealism which is often a characteristic of the final stages of war, that the necessity for the introduction of a scheme of continued education of the adolescent received national recognition. Technical education was not mentioned specifically in the 1944 Act, but was included in the much broader heading of 'further education'. Once more, an Act of Parliament proclaimed compulsory further education:

'. . . it shall be the duty of every local education authority to secure the provision for their area of adequate facilities for further education, that is to say:

'(a) full-time and part-time education for persons over compulsory school age; and
'(b) leisure-time occupation in such organized cultural training and recreative activities as are suited to their requirements, for any persons over compulsory school age who are able and willing to profit by the facilities provided for that purpose.'[7]

The visionary 'day continuation schools' of the 1918 Act were revived once more and transformed into county colleges. They were to be attended by all youngsters in employment aged fifteen to eighteen:

'. . . It shall be the duty of every local education authority to establish and maintain county colleges, that is to say, centres approved by the Minister for providing for young persons who are not in full-time attendance at any school or other educational institution such further education, including physical, practical, and vocational training, as will enable them to develop their various aptitudes and capacities and will prepare them for the responsibilities of citizenship.[8]

'. . . The requirements specified in a college attendance notice shall be such as to secure the attendance of the person upon whom it is served at a county college –

'(a) for one whole day, or two half-days, in each of forty-four weeks in every year while he remains a young person; or
'(b) where the authority are satisfied that the continuous attendance would be more suitable in the case of that young person, for one continuous period of eight weeks, or two continuous periods of four weeks in every such year.'[9]

The local education authorities were to submit plans for the provision of county colleges in their area, and, after 1 April 1947 it was to become their duty to establish and maintain county colleges.

After more than twenty years these laws have not come to fruition and England still remains without some system of compulsory parttime education for young people under eighteen. How much longer are we to persist in this folly of passing laws and of ignoring them, of refusing to *insist* that all young people be given the opportunity to improve themselves both in their capacity as workers and as citizens in a democracy? At the beginning of the century Kerschensteiner achieved far more than we have done until now, for, whereas in England we are still at the stage of discussions and plans and laws, he progressed to the stage of *action* and saw that his plans were *put into force*.

SELECTION AND EFFICIENCY

Vocational training in modern society is not merely an educational necessity, but is also a demand imposed by the workings of the economy of the modern industrial state, where an ever-increasing job specialization manoeuvres the balance of the industrial scene. The growing demand for skilled and specialized workers makes recognized courses of training in the various skills and trades imperative.

Not only should the worker receive training in his chosen occupation, but he should also receive such a superlative training that he becomes what Kerschensteiner called a 'Qualitätsarbeiter' – a worker who is satisfied only with work of quality. Pride in work, which is determined by success and efficiency, is the hall-mark of every good and conscientious worker and is a quality which, by tradition, Germany holds in particular esteem. Pride and efficiency in work will grow best where there is a combination of understanding, aptitude, and will in the worker. Only under these conditions will he really exert himself to achieve a high standard of work, or, in other words: 'Industrial efficiency can only be fully achieved with a satisfied labour force, and this, in turn, depends on each individual employee doing a job suited to him and which he has been helped by systematic training to perform competently and confidently.'[10]

If the worker is to take pride in his work, not only must he be employed in an occupation to which he is suited by nature and aptitude and in which he can use his talents to their best advantage but also it is essential that he have an inner sense of involvement in his work. This sense of involvement will be stimulated if the worker is made aware of the specific role which his particular job of work plays in relation to the other occupations in the enterprise. It has been shown that the young German workers are given regular teaching along these lines at their vocational school. They learn about the different stages in the manufacturing process, how the firm is organized and the factors which determine its success. They are made to feel not as isolated individuals but as part of a community, which is composed of people of all ages and abilities all working together at a common task.

The high percentage pass rate at the German apprenticeship examinations (90 per cent of the apprentices pass these final examinations) can be partly attributed to the comprehensive advisory and selective system in use in Germany. For forty years now, there has been a careers advisory service which is consulted by most school-leavers. Some of the larger firms employ their own psychologist who interviews and tests candidates before a contract of apprenticeship is entered upon. This selective system, whether it be made through the careers advisory service, or through the individual firms, sorts out the unsuitable candidates from the very beginning, and further sifting of workers is carried out during the apprenticeship, of which the first three months is regarded as being a trial period.[11]

This flexibility, characteristic of the German apprenticeship system, and so lacking in our own, facilitates the placing of youngsters in the trade which corresponds best to their individual abilities and interests, and where they are therefore likely to give of their best. The German scheme also offers flexibility with regard to the age of entry into an apprenticeship, although individual firms may have their own regulations in this matter. The lack of age limit for entry into an apprenticeship permits those who, for some reason, did not take up an apprenticeship immediately on leaving school, to do so later. (Apprenticeship in Germany may begin as soon as the youngster leaves school, whereas the age of entry in England is fifteen years for some trades, sixteen for others and not all trades have arrangements permitting later entry, even with higher educational qualifications which have been gained by staying at school a little longer.)

ECONOMIC TRENDS AND TECHNICAL TRAINING

Increasing specialization and suppression of certain trades demand, too, that there should be facilities for the training and retraining of adults[12] and that the training, which is given both to adults and youngsters, should be equal to the demands of industry. For some years government training centres have been established in the United Kingdom to tackle the problem of training adults who have no skilled trade and others who wish to undertake retraining in another skill. Here, it is essential that we should make sure that we are not still training for occupations which are, or shortly will be, outdated. In this respect the Man-power Research Unit of the Ministry of Labour has a significant role to play. This unit was established in 1963 with the task of ascertaining the man-power requirements of the various sectors of the economy and of assisting in the planning of industrial training.

In Germany, the German Executive for the Technical School System had been founded as early as 1908 to examine the requirements of industry with regard to the supply of suitably trained operatives. With the years, the scope of the Executive increased and at the present time the regulations regarding apprenticeship training for industry are determined by the Executive's modern counterpart, the Central Office for Vocational Training, situated in Bonn. This office compiles trade classifications, that is, it prepares descriptions of jobs, lays down and standardizes the training necessary for each trade and *requires every apprentice to fill in a weekly report card on the work he has done*. The job descriptions are compiled after consultation with the various trade associations, chambers of industry or commerce, employers' associations, and trade unions. They must be sent for approval to the Federal Ministry of Economics and the Ministry of Labour, before they can become classified trades. *If visiting representatives from the respective chambers find that a firm lacks the training facilities which have been laid down by the Central Office, they have the power to deny the firm the right to take on apprentices.*

The larger firms usually provide special training workshops for their apprentices (according to the latest figures, there are about two thousand of these special workshops for apprentices in the Federal Republic), or, if this is not possible, a corner of an existing workshop is set aside for apprentice training. The smaller firms send their apprentices to a communal workshop. The apprentices work under the supervision of a qualified instructor, who is usually a 'master.' As a rule, about twenty apprentices work under one supervisor, and, in their first year at least, do not normally work on production, although this does vary from firm to firm.

Thus it has been shown that Germany has taken steps to ensure that the training of apprentices is tackled seriously and that both the content and length of training in each trade are standardized for the whole country. The German apprentice can therefore be sure of receiving a sound factory-based practical training combined with the more formal trade and general education which he receives at the vocational school.

FOLK HIGH SCHOOLS

However, learning and apprenticeship do not end with the passing of the final examination, as Kerschensteiner well realized when he introduced his voluntary courses for journeymen. The role of the German technical schools in fulfilling the worker's desire for more knowledge has already been pointed out, but also the splendid work of the German Volkshochschule, Folk High School, cannot be passed without comment. This institution, well established in Germany, is a vital driving force in the intellectual and social life in the towns. The schools aim at fulfilling and furthering the desire for knowledge and at promoting a broader interest in life, by means of a variety of courses on a wide selection of vocational, academic, and cultural subjects. Besides the wide provision of weekly courses, there are also week-end courses or programmes of longer duration, which take place in pleasant country surroundings. Study trips abroad may also be arranged through the Folk High School.

In his prize essay, Kerschensteiner had pointed to the work being achieved by non-vocational, evening courses in England and had stressed the importance of providing such facilities in Germany too, so that the door to education was *always* open to every age group. There is no doubt that the Volkshochschule fulfils many of Kerschensteiner's ideals, for it is a stimulus and source of interest to over six million Germans who participate in its work. The courses are led by specialists in the various fields of study and the help of university staff is often enlisted for the public lectures which are arranged regularly.[13]

In connexion with this rather informal educational work, the splendid work being achieved in some of the German workers' hostels, built since the last war in an attempt to help solve the acute housing shortage, must also be mentioned here. These hostels for young people have mostly been founded by the churches and other voluntary organizations and some of them, aware of the pedagogical tasks which they can accomplish, set up courses of various kinds in the evenings, where the youngsters come together in a community spirit and are actively engaged in common pursuits. The courses are usually of a cultural nature and promote active and intelligent use of leisure time.

For those people with purely academic interests, the door to university study remains open. The foreign visitor to Germany is always impressed by the number of older people sitting in the crowded lecture halls, listening as intently as their younger fellow students to lectures, and sometimes discussions, on all manner of subjects.

The above-mentioned aspects of education illustrate how Kerschensteiner's principle that the desire to learn should always be encouraged and promoted, is being achieved in numerous ways in present-day Germany. Facilities for further education are available at all stages of life and achievement.

KERSCHENSTEINER'S PHILOSOPHICAL STUDIES

While Kerschensteiner did much to further the education of the general public, he is, with justice, best known as 'father of the vocational school'. His inspiring work in this field has already been discussed extensively and needs no further comment at this stage. However, there remains one more aspect of his work and thought which must be considered, if a true portrayal of the man himself is to be achieved. This last aspect covers the final stage in Kerschensteiner's life, when he occupied himself with a search for a philosophical and theoretical justification of his life's work in the vocational schools.

Kerschensteiner's first theoretical works, apart from his earlier prize essay, had appeared in the years immediately following the implementation of his plans for the reorganization of the old continuation schools. Before this period, his time had been fully occupied in work on the practical aspects of the organization of the schools and he had had no time to devote himself to a study of the theoretical basis of education. It was a well-known fact that when he came to office, Kerschensteiner had read very few of the great educational thinkers.

In addition to devoting much time to the writing of books and to his own private reading, Kerschensteiner found that his time was also claimed by other matters, for in 1911 he had been elected to parliament by the liberals. The regular trips by train to Berlin exerted pressures on his time, energy, and health. In 1915, on their thirtieth wedding anniversary, his wife Sophie died after a long illness. The loss of his wife and the onset of the First World War, in which his three sons fought for the cause of the Fatherland, were contributory factors to the period of great strain to which Kerschensteiner was subjected at this time.

THE CULTURAL HERITAGE AND EDUCATION

The opportunity to let himself be absorbed into an academic atmosphere and to take up a serious study of educational philosophy was finally afforded him in 1919 when he retired from his position as Munich's Director of Education. In the previous year he had accepted a post as honorary Professor of Pedagogy at Munich University, where the work gave him a great deal of pleasure.

A field of educational philosophy hitherto untreated by Kerschensteiner, was dealt with at length in his book, *The Fundamentals of the Educational Process and their Consequences for School Organization*,[14] which was published in 1917. In this book, and in his later works, Kerschensteiner laid considerable emphasis on the role which the 'objects of our cultural heritage' ('Kulturgüter') could play in the educative process. Here Kerschensteiner was greatly concerned with the idea of man being surrounded by products of a cultural heritage, which embodied the ideas and thoughts of men in a particular civilization in the past; the living man should learn to recognize the 'value' embodied in these things. He must not live surrounded by them, unaware and unappreciative of their true value and meaning, ignoring the reason and spirit which lay behind their existence. All these products of civilization were initially a product of man's mind, spirit, and outlook on life and all were impregnated with the values which he held in esteem. Customs, Christianity, Buddhism, music, poetry, laws, and constitutions were all such products of civilization and all of them testified to man's spiritual and mental outlook at a certain period of history. They should not merely be accepted objectively for what they were in themselves, but should be appreciated for the idea or 'value' which they represented.

Kerschensteiner considered that these cultural possessions and manifestations of past ages could only begin to have real educational worth when the onlooker sank into an active and meaningful contemplation of their innate spiritual and moral 'values.' The process of true education was reached when the individual progressed beyond the stage when he was concerned purely with a theoretical analysis of the 'values' represented by the particular object under consideration. He was involved in the process of true education when he became drawn to the 'value' itself and was able to experience that same 'value' in his own mind and soul with a burning intensity. Real education was concerned with the formation of a system of 'values', by means of a rich experience of the various monuments of our heritage which surrounded us: 'Education in its broadest sense . . . is the formation of the soul by means of the objective civilization which surrounds us.'[15]

Kerschensteiner stressed that a cultural possession only became an educative factor when the soul which contemplated it had a bond of sympathy to it and had a similar structure of its own. A person who was in no way musical would fail to perceive the beauty inherent in a Beethoven symphony. In the same way, a person whose mental and spiritual make-up favoured practical things would never truly experience the 'value' offered by some object which had a theoretical nature. It was essential that the structure of the object under consideration be of a similar structure to the soul of the onlooker, for only under these conditions could the individual penetrate into deep communion with the 'values' embodied in the object and feel the joy and ecstacy of self-identification with that 'value'. Thus, a mere appreciation of the 'value' was not enough; the individual must have as deep and as intensive experience of it as possible in his own heart and soul. For, 'Education is the individual formation of a sense of values, inspired by the manifestations of our cultural heritage.'[16]

In his later works Kerschensteiner treated the structure of the soul in greater detail. One of the basic themes in his earlier outlook on education had been that, above all, the citizen must be 'useful' to society, that he must be performing 'useful' work which could contribute to the welfare of the community. However, in this later philosophical stage of his life, Kerschensteiner no longer laid the stress on the 'usefulness' of the citizen (although he still supported this theory), but stressed instead the principle that the citizen should be engaged in work for which he had an inner vocation. He was to carry out some kind of work to which his soul felt attracted, where there was some corresponding bond between the structure of the individual's soul, his mental and spiritual outlook, and the structure and qualities of the work. Education would be effected while the individual was engaged in work for which he had an inner calling or vocation: 'Only by carrying out work for which we have an inner vocation, can we attain pure humanity.'[17]

Even during Kerschensteiner's lifetime this precept met with direct criticism and it was protested that, while there were some creative professions for which one could very well have an inner calling, there existed a great number of unskilled occupations to which the worker could not possibly feel any sense of vocation. This has an even wider application in the modern age of automation, where many jobs, although perhaps demanding a certain amount of basic skill or knowledge, are of a purely routine and repetitive nature. Here, Kerschensteiner's answer was that if it was impossible for a man to have a vocation for his work, because this was of a simple, mechanical nature, there still remained one aspect of human life and activity to which every man had a calling: this was man's gregarious nature and his instinct to be a social being. Therefore, in cases where there was no calling to the chosen occupation, Kerschensteiner's continuation schools were to concentrate even more on developing the individual's talents as a member of society and of a community.

Throughout his life, Kerschensteiner's basic principle regarding the aim of education remained constant – to educate the individual to be a man of sound moral character, who would display firm moral courage and a feeling of responsibility towards his fellow men. The formation of citizens and the formation of *men* were really one and the same thing, for, 'Just as there can be no true community without true men, in the same way, one cannot educate people to be men without educating them to be a community.'[18] Every member of the community should endeavour to contribute to the increasing welfare and moral progress of that community. The individual would consciously aim at achieving this in a number of ways: 'The individual works at the moral progress of the community partly by his sheer mental activity, partly by his professional work, and finally, partly in his assertion of his desire for justice, which is expressed in his active participation in the political life of the community.'[19]

In 1921 appeared Kerschensteiner's book on the qualities of the teacher, *The Soul of the Educator and the Problem of Teacher Training*[20] – a fascinating work, impregnated with the author's own love of life, love of children, and love of the 'values' which governed his actions. In this book he distinguished the true teachers, the ones who were character-

Into the Future · 133

ized by a love towards their pupils, from those who were engaged in 'pseudo-pedagogical' acts, i.e. those whose will to teach sprang from egoistic motives. The real educator was the one who found his soul's greatest satisfaction in moulding the growing child, who, in turn, would himself be later a bearer of those eternal 'values' in which the educator was such an ardent believer.

Kerschensteiner's last years brought some measure of happiness into his life again, for he had remarried, and, freed from the worries and strains of his work connected with educational administration, he could dedicate himself to his now passionate study of educational theory. He also continued to give public lectures, and on several occasions was asked to help in the reorganization of foreign educational systems (in 1926 he was asked to advise on matters concerning vocational education in the Irish Free State, but he declined the offer). However, he usually preferred to stay in his beloved Munich, seeking companionship among his friends and in his music.

In 1924 Kerschensteiner published his *Authority and Freedom as Educational Principles*,[21] and in 1926 he published the fruits of twelve years of work and thinking, his *Theory of Education*.[22] In this huge treatise on the philosophy of education he set out his general theories on man and his education. Once more the concept of the eternal values of morality, truth, holiness, beauty, duty, etc., took up a dominant part in his discussions on education and life. Education had nothing to do with the accumulation of facts and knowledge, but was concerned with the highest possible development of the individual's mental, spiritual, and bodily powers, and with his recognition of his own ability to fulfil 'values' and to contribute to the welfare of the community. Kerschensteiner's last work, his *Theory of Educational Organization*[23] was published after his death.

KERSCHENSTEINER'S VALIDITY TODAY

Kerschensteiner was one of the few educationists fortunate enough to see the fruits of their plans during their own lifetime. The reorganization of vocational education and the recognition of its necessity had been effected long before his death in 1932, although lack of funds and ruptures caused by the First World War had prevented the full implementation of Kerschensteiner's proposals. Yet, despite the dynamic success of the vocational schools, there remained several aspects of

Kerschensteiner's educational organization which Germany itself failed to put into practice, although similar steps have been taken in countries outside Germany.

One of these schemes which Kerschensteiner proposed was the introduction of a technical grammar school, an idea which Germany has refused to take up, although such schools form an integral part of the educational system in France, for instance. Another of Kerschensteiner's theories which has been stressed more abroad than in his homeland is the principle that the child should learn as much as possible from his environment; in consequence, the curriculum in schools should bear a very strong and real connexion with the demands of life. It will be remembered that, in this respect, Kerschensteiner introduced handicrafts into the curriculum of the elementary school. The most recent and dramatic attempt to make schooling correspond more to the actual needs of life was effected in the 1958 Russian educational reforms, which declared as their aims the strengthening of the connexion between school and life. In all general secondary education study of and participation in production was required of all pupils between the ages of fifteen and eighteen up to one-third of the school time. The full secondary education was extended into an eleventh year at the same time and we may ourselves regard this as academic compensation for the time taken from the academic studies. During the school year 1964 to 1965, however, much of this was abandoned and, at least in some places, complete secondary schooling ended at the tenth year.[24] Industrial orientation is also a feature of the new Swedish comprehensive school, where, in the eighth grade, the pupils spend three weeks in various places of work, in order that they may gain some experience of working in different occupations.

Since Kerschensteiner first set about the reorganization of the old continuation schools, the role of the worker has changed considerably, and therefore it is not possible to take over his ideas in their entirety and to superimpose them 'en bloc' on to any system of further education which may evolve in England. Kerschensteiner's new system was born essentially of the last years of the craft age, where the worker or craftsman was in charge of a task of work right from its commencement to its very completion and would therefore take pride in work well done. In the modern working world, however, where thousands of workers are employed in just one concern and increasing specializa-

Into the Future · 135

tion demands the delegation of work, it is impossible for the worker to handle the product at every stage of its manufacture. Despite this basic difference which distinguishes today's worker from the craftsman, the modern worker can nevertheless be trained to have a similar sense of involvement in his work. Even if the low level of skill – or complete lack of it – required in the occupation gives the industrial employee little opportunity to experience a sense of achievement or pride in work, his sense of involvement can be aroused if he is made increasingly aware of the relevance and value of his own particular work for the completion of the finished article.

Kerschensteiner's schools gave trade instruction, but it was trade instruction of a fairly broad nature; yet, the more specialized industrial processes become, the more specialized must be the training given to employees. So the criterion today may well be not, as for Kerschensteiner, that trade specialization should be brought into the continuation schools, but instead, that we should take care that, once having introduced trade training, we do not *overspecialize* in the vocational schools.

The question of how to rehumanize the work of the vocational schools is an eager discussion point in present-day Germany. Does the solution to this problem lie in the introduction of a more liberal timetable in the schools? Should the curriculum be broadened to include music and art appreciation (as it does in some of the German vocational schools), and should it on principle devote more time to teaching the students how best to use their leisure time, which, with the advent of the shorter working week, will continue to increase? Or, alternatively, does a liberal education consist of giving a broader base to trade education? A broader trade education would certainly enable the student to be more flexible and adaptable in his skills, in the event of his own trade becoming outdated.

The modern industrial scene presents, on the one hand, a picture of energetic expansion and rising output, and, on the other, insecurity and instability for the worker, who may find that efficient planning methods and new inventions are driving his occupation out of the market. It is clear that there is here a real and urgent need for an efficient system of trade forecasting, which will ensure that young people do not continue to receive training in occupations for which the future holds no scope. At the same time, a broader technical training is indicated, which will enable the worker to transfer more easily from one trade to another. It is interesting here to note that if an English firm has to reduce the number of its operatives, the newest members to the firm are the most likely to suffer, while in Germany, where the apprenticeship examination is marked in grades, the workers with the lowest grades are the ones who leave first. The knowledge that the grade obtained in the apprenticeship examination can have a bearing on the rest of the worker's career also acts as a stimulus to the young apprentice.

With the inevitable changes in future labour trends, it is essential not only that the basic training be suited to the needs of industry but also that more vocational training courses be set up, both to keep the worker abreast of current trends and developments in his own trade and to provide complete retraining in another trade. Here use could be made of our numerous university and college buildings which stand idle during the long vacations: in America wide use is made of these buildings for instruction in all kinds of vocational training courses.

COMPULSORY FURTHER EDUCATION

Kerschensteiner's pioneering work led to the eventual introduction of compulsory vocational education for *all* German youngsters between the compulsory school leaving age and the age of eighteen. England, however, presents a very different picture: in England and Wales the total number of all those released from their employment in 1964 to take part-time courses was 574,268. Less than half of these – 275,604 – were young people under the age of eighteen, which is the age group of young people in Germany undergoing compulsory further education. The young people under eighteen who attend courses on a day-release basis in this country constitute only 19·0 per cent of the total working population in that age group. 31·0 per cent of all young male workers are released from their employment, and only 7·3 per cent of the girls under eighteen are released. Compared with Germany where there is compulsory further education for *all* youngsters, the situation in England is indeed a wretched one.

The Henniker-Heaton Committee,[25] which was set up in order to study what steps could be taken to bring about an increase in the number of young people engaged in further education on a day-release basis, aimed at doubling the present number on day-release by 1969–70.

This would entail an annual increase of 50,000. The report was concerned solely with the first of Crowther's three stages in the organization of compulsory further education, i.e. with the extension of the present voluntary system.

According to the Henniker-Heaton proposals, special opportunities for day-release were to be accorded to those youngsters who had already shown an interest in further education by attending evening-only vocational courses: more facilities were also to be provided for those youngsters who did not require specifically vocational education. Local education authorities were to give a lead in further schemes for day-release and local targets were to be, and have been set up, for the increase in numbers of those participating in day-release courses. The report also established that for the extra 250,000 day-release students, which the committee had set as the national target, more than 5,000 additional teachers would be required.

The Crowther Committee had proposed that the introduction of compulsory attendance should then follow in chosen regional areas, after the basic school-leaving age had been raised to sixteen. However, Dr Downer, in his paper delivered to the British Association, has pointed out that if the timing of Crowther's suggestions are carried out, England will not see the third stage, compulsory education for all, until the 1980s, whereas Newsom requires it to be available from the mid 1970s. For, if the education of the Newsom child is to be re-orientated, it is equally important that he should not break his links with education at the age of sixteen but should then automatically go on to part-time education.

The National Federation of Professional Workers, in their report 'Day Release for Clerical Workers', wants an assurance to be given that compulsory further education will be granted not later than 1975. They feel that Henniker-Heaton has overlooked their workers, for 'the clerical workers constitute the largest occupational group who generally have not been afforded day-release in the past and at the same time are by far the largest group of those who have attended evening vocational courses in their own time.'[26] They therefore wish that 'as from 1970–71 every young worker under the age of eighteen who is not granted day-release voluntarily by his employer . . . will be legally entitled to claim the right to day-release'.[27] With the implementation of this proposal, the writers feel that the demand for further education would exceed Henniker-Heaton's targets, and that, therefore, the targets for the increase of the number of youngsters engaged in further education should be raised from 250,000 to 460,000 by 1969–70.

With the introduction of the Industrial Training Act in 1964, a great step forward was made, for here the government committed itself in the question of technical training. The Act provides for the setting up of industrial training boards, which:

'(a) shall provide or secure the provision of such courses and other facilities ... for the training of persons employed or intending to be employed in the industry as may be required, having regard to any course or facilities otherwise available to such persons,' and,

'(c) shall from time to time consider such employments in the industry as appear to require consideration and publish recommendations with regard to the nature and length of the training for any such employment and the further education to be associated with the training, the persons by and to whom the training ought to be given, the standards to be attained as a result of the training and the methods of ascertaining whether those standards have been attained'.

'(d) may apply and make arrangements for the application of selection tests or other methods of ascertaining the attainment of any standards recommended by the board and may award certificates of the attainment of those standards'.[28]

This Act is restrictive in its proposals, in that it does not yet embrace compulsory training. Though it is a great step forward in the history of industrial training, it is still only the first step on the road to further education for all. Further education for *all*, as defined in the 1944 Act, whether they be the brighter boys and girls or the Newsom youngsters, boys in industry or girls in clerical offices, remains our objective. It is bound to be achieved at some point in the future, but our concern should be that further education for all is introduced *at the earliest date possible*.

Notes

CHAPTER I

1 See M. R. Heafford, *Pestalozzi and his Relevance Today*, Methuen, 1966.
2 The Gymnasium is the classical grammar school, modelled on the ideas of Wilhelm von Humboldt at the beginning of the nineteenth century, and prepares its pupils for the Abitur, which is the university matriculation certificate.
3 Max Karl Ludwig Planck, 1858–1947, was awarded the Nobel Prize for Physics in 1918 for his work on the quantum theory. In 1926 he was elected as a foreign member of the Royal Society in London. In 1930 he became president of the Kaiser-Wilhelm Society for Scientific Research, which after the war was renamed the Max Planck Society. The Max Planck Society now has forty-eight research institutes in the Federal Republic.
4 Paul Gordan, *Vorlesungen über Invariantentheorie*, Teubner, Leipzig, 1885–7.
5 Quoted by Marie Kerschensteiner in *Georg Kerschensteiner, Lebensweg eines Schulreformers*, p. 123, Oldenbourg, 1954.
6 Stadtschulrat: this post also included the 'Amt des königlichen Schulkommissärs'.

CHAPTER 2

1 *Beobachtungen zur Theorie des Lehrplanes*.
2 Directives quoted by S. Thyssen on p. 16 of *Die Berufsschule in Idee und Gestaltung*, Girardet, Essen, 1954: 'The schoolmasters are also to be put under the obligation diligently to teach the youth of the district, even if they are not their own pupils, and to practise with them the catechism and singing. This instruction shall take place after the catechism and shall be held in the churches in the summer, and in the schoolrooms in the winter.'
3 Quoted on p. 16 of *Fünf Jahrzehnte berufsbildendes Schulwesen in Württemberg*, published by the Deutscher Verband der Gewerbelehrer, Landesverband Württemberg e. V. Holland & Josenhans Verlag, Stuttgart.
4 August Hermann Francke, 1663–1727, one of the founders of the

University of Halle in 1694. He also introduced a seminary for the training of teachers and a small school for the poor, as well as other educational establishments. He founded the 'Pädagogium' in Halle in 1696, where he revolutionized the curriculum by introducing such new subjects as modern languages, sciences, and handwork. Experiments, demonstrations, and visits to observe craftsmen in their workshops were essential features in the teaching. Johann Juluis Hecker, 1707–68, carried Francke's ideas farther and established an 'ökonomisch-mathematische Realschule' in Berlin, with the 'useful' subjects at the centre of the curriculum, which would prepare the pupils for their future vocation. An enthusiastic revival of the foundation of Realschulen took place in the second half of the nineteenth century. They have now mostly been transformed into 'middle schools'.

5 Karl Wilhelm von Humboldt, 1767–1835, philologist and historian, sometime Minister of Education in Prussia. Humboldt's views on the necessity that the secondary schools should impart a 'liberal' education found considerable support in England in the second half of the nineteenth century. He saw the task of the secondary schools as being to give an education which would enable the pupils to gain appreciation of and inspiration from studies of the classics and of ancient Greece. At the same time, he insisted on the introduction into the curriculum of certain general subjects which would ensure that the pupils also received a sound general culture.

CHAPTER 3

1 *Betrachtungen zur Theorie des Lehrplanes*, p. 9, Gerber, 1899.
2 Op. cit., p. 11.
3 Johann Friedrich Herbart, 1776–1841, Professor of Philosophy and Pedagogy at Königsberg university: a practical educator as well as an educational theorist. His psychological and philosophical studies provided an assessment of man's soul and mind, of the processes of thought and learning, of the aims of education and of the methods and subjects to be stressed in the attainment of these aims. Herbart's philosophy of education found ready acceptance throughout Germany, and his ideas, especially those relating to theories of interest, received considerable attention in England and America at the end of the nineteenth century.
4 *Betrachtungen zur Theorie des Lehrplanes*, p. 13, Gerber, 1899.
5 *Staatsbürgerliche Erziehung der deutschen Jugend*, 5th ed., p. 12, Villaret, 1911.
6 See H. Becker, *German Youth, Bond or Free*, Routledge, 1948; Hans Kohn, *The Mind of Germany: the Education of a Nation*, Macmillan, 1961; Roy Pascal, 'Nationalism and the German Intellectuals', *The German Mind and Outlook*, Chapman and Hall, 1945; G. W. D. Hopwood: 'The Intellectual Forerunners of National Socialism', M. Ed. thesis, University of Reading, 1964.

Notes · 141

7 The Wandervögel, under the leadership of Karl Fischer, was a group of young people who rebelled against the intellectualism in the schools and who sought to revive the concept of the simple life in harmony with nature. They formed rambling groups and revived old German folk-songs and customs.

8 *Begriff der Arbeitsschule*, 6th ed., p. 11, Teubner, 1925.

9 *Staatsbürgerliche Erziehung der deutschen Jugend*, 5th ed., p. 13, Villaret, 1911.

10 'Berufs- oder Allgemeinbildung?', first published in the *Pädagogische Reform*, 1904, no. 1. Also contained in *Grundfragen der Schulorganisation*.

11 Contained in the introduction to *Organisation und Lehrpläne der obligatorischen Fach- und Fortbildungsschulen für Knaben in München*, Gerber, 1910.

12 *Begriff der Arbeitsschule*, 6th edn., pp. 19–21, Teubner, 1925.

13 *Staatsbürgerliche Erziehung der deutschen Jugend*, 5th edn, p. 15, Villaret, 1911.

14 See *Aristotle's Thought on Education and its Relevance for Today* by C. E. Winn and M. L. Jacks, Methuen, 1966.

15 *Staatsbürgerliche Erziehung der deutschen Jugend*, 5th edn, pp. 16–18, Villaret, 1911.

16 *Betrachtungen zur Theorie des Lehrplanes* p. 18, Gerber, 1899.

17 'Heimatkunde' – regional studies – is a subject which occupies a traditional and important place in the German school curriculum. It aims at increasing the pupils' knowledge of local affairs, history, and geography, and promotes regional pride and patriotism. Past history has shown, however, that, at times, the scope of the teaching of 'Heimatkunde' in Germany has been extended so as to embrace patriotism, not only on the local level but also on the larger, national level. Details of how 'Heimatkunde' has, in the past, even been used to encourage an open nationalism are shown in 'Nationalism in German Schools', by Kathleen Southwell Davis, *The Educational Forum*, May 1954.

18 'Berufs- oder Allgemeinbildung?', first published in 1904. Included in *Grundfragen der Schulorganisation*.

CHAPTER 4

1 *Theorie der Bildung*, p. 263, Teubner, 1926.

2 *Staatbürgerliche Erziehung der deutschen Jugend* 5th edn, p. 35, Villaret, 1911.

3 Op. cit., p. 33.

4 Op. cit., pp. 35–6.

5 Op. cit., p. 40.

6 *Charakterbegriff und Charaktererziehung*.

7 *Charakterbegriff und Charaktererziehung*, p. 86, Teubner, 1912.

8 Op. cit., p. 97.

9 'Die Arbeitsschule' in German means literally the 'work-school', and has been translated into English as the 'industrial school' (by Pinter, *The Idea of the Industrial School*, 1913). However, this translation conveys the impression that

the work undertaken in this school was purely of a technical or vocational nature – which was not the case. By 'Arbeit' here Kerschensteiner meant the child's active, intellectual participation in the learning process, whatever form that learning took on. I have therefore translated 'Arbeitsschule' not as 'work-school' but as 'activity school'. In this connexion, 'activity' for Kerschensteiner could include physical or manual work, but the significant point about the term was that it *necessarily* embraced intellectual effort.

Kerschensteiner intended to apply the principles of the 'activity school' to the elementary school and the continuation school.

10 *Staatsbürgerliche Erziehung der deutschen Jugend* 5th edn, p. 38, Villaret, 1911.
11 Op. cit., p. 39.
12 'Das Problem der Volkserziehung', first published 1908. Included in *Grundfragen der Schulorganisation*.
13 'Berufs- oder Allgemeinbildung?', first published 1904. Also in *Grundfragen der Schulorganisation*.

CHAPTER 5

1 'Die drei Grundlagen für die Organisation des Fortbildungsschulwesens', speech delivered in Munich on 7 October 1906. Also contained in *Grundfragen der Schulorganisation*.
2 Introduction to *Organisation und Lehrpläne der obligatorischen Fach- und Fortbilbungsschulen für Knaben in München*, Gerber, 1910.
3 *Staatsbürgerliche Erziehung der deutschen Jugend*, 5th edn, p. 34, Villaret, 1911.
4 Sir Richard Livingstone, *Education for a World Adrift*, p. 60, Cambridge University Press, 1949.
5 'Die drei Grundlagen für die Organisation des Fortbildungsschulwesens', speech delivered in 1906. Contained in *Grundfragen der Schulorganisation*.
6 *Staatsbürgerliche Erziehung der deutschen Jugend*, 5th edn, pp. 52-4, Villaret, 1911.
7 Op. cit., pp. 69-70.
8 Kerschensteiner was a staunch supporter of the country boarding-schools (Landerziehungsheime) which had already been established by Hermann Lietz (1868–1919), who was assistant master at Abbotsholme School, Derbyshire, from 1896 to 1898. These schools aimed at giving the pupils the opportunity to develop in a community spirit, surrounded by the beauty and calm of nature. The schools endeavoured to unfold *all* the manifold talents and aptitudes of the pupils – regarding academic work as being but one feature of their educational tasks. See Herman Lietz, 'Emlohstobba: Fiction or Fact?', *Abbotsholme*, ed. Cecil Reddie, George Allen, 1900.
9 'Die Neugestaltung des gewerblichen Schulwesens in München', speech delivered in 1902. Also contained in *Grundfragen der Schulorganisation*.

10 In 1965-6 there were 1,029 British Voluntary Service workers in the underdeveloped countries, the majority of whom were working in the field of education. Of these 1,029 volunteers, only 61 had technical or industrial qualifications.
11 Lord Robertson of Oakridge, *Hansard*, p. 1140, March 1965.
12 'Die Schule der Zukunft: eine Arbeitsschule', speech given in Zürich at the anniversary celebrations of Pestalozzi. Also contained in *Grundfragen der Schulorganisation*.

CHAPTER 6

1 *Beobachtungen und Vergleiche über Einrichtungen für gewerbliche Erziehung ausserhalb Bayerns*, Gerber, 1901.
2 See *Report of the Consultative Committee on Secondary Education with special reference to Grammar Schools and Technical High Schools* (Spens, H.M.S.O., 1938), Chapter 4. paras. 6, 11, 18: '. . . The studies of the ordinary secondary school should be brought into closer contact than at present with the practical affairs of life.' See also *A Report of the Central Advisory Council for Education* (Newsom, H.M.S.O., 1963), Chapter 14, para. 317: 'Most boys and girls, and especially those with whom we are concerned, want their education to be practical and realistic. They feel a good deal better if they can see that it is vocational.' See also Chapter 14, para. 324, and chapters 5 and 17.
3 Quoted in 'Berufs- oder Allgemeinbildung?', 1904. Also contained in *Grundfragen der Schulorganisation*.
4 The French law on school reorganization, passed on 6 January 1959, has similar aims in view and raises the minimum school-leaving age to sixteen (to take effect from 1967). This reform includes the reorganization of the teaching given to the least academic pupils in their last three years at school, which will now be placed on a more practical basis. A choice of specialization may be made from the following: agriculture (agriculture and housecraft for girls), rural studies, and urban work. General studies will also be pursued.
5 Note the excellent work being undertaken in the French *écoles normales d'apprentissage* which were introduced in 1946 to train teachers in the *collèges d'enseignement technique* (at that time called *centres d'apprentissage*). The outstanding feature of these technical teacher-training courses is the emphasis which is laid on training the students in the art of teaching. A study of the psychology of adolescence, of the learning process and teaching methods are all essential factors in the course: the students' technical and general knowledge is also furthered. The course lasts one year and is terminated by a written examination plus a practical teaching practice.
6 'Die Neugestaltung des gewerblichen Schulwesens in München', speech delivered in 1902. Also included in the *Grundfragen der Schulorganisation*.

7 *Die Entwicklung der zeichnerischen Begabung*, Gerber.
8 *Wesen und Wert des naturwissenschaftlichen Unterrichts*, Teubner.
9 See Sir Cyril Burt: 'Transfer of Training', *Educational Review*, vol. 12, no. 2, February 1960, published by Birmingham Univ. Institute of Education.
10 These views bear similarity to Kerschensteiner's views on the value of a study of the ancient classics. His ideas on the value and function of modern languages in the secondary schools would not be acceptable to modern educationists, for whom comparative studies are an essential feature in language teaching, as well as oral work, both of which scarcely find a recognized place in Kerschensteiner's system.
11 *Die staatsbürgerliche Erziehung der deutschen Jugend*, Villaret.
12 *Grundfragen der Schulorganisation*, Teubner.
13 *Organisation und Lehrpläne der obligatorischen Fach- und Fortbildungsschulen für Knaben in München*, Gerber.
14 *Der Begriff der staatsbürgerlichen Erziehung*, Teubner.
15 *Charakterbegriff und Charaktererziehung*, Teubner.
16 *Der Begriff der Arbeitsschule*, Teubner.
17 *Die zeitgemässe Ausgestaltung der Mädchenfortbildungsschule*,' lecture given in 1902. Also contained in *Grundfragen der Schulorganisation*.
18 Following a law passed in 1941, a similar type of instruction has been introduced in France, called *l'enseignement postscolaire agricole-ménager*.
19 *Landwirtschaftlicher Beruf und staatsbürgerliche Erziehung*', Lecture given in 1910, first published 1912. Also contained in *Grundfragen der Schulorganisation*.

CHAPTER 7

1 *Lehr- und Bildungsplan für die gewerblichen Berufsschulen Baden-Württembergs*, April 1962.
2 Op. cit.
3 'Land' is the German term for each state within the Federal Republic.
4 *Lehr- und Bildunsplan für die gewerblichen Berufsschulen Baden-Württembergs*, April 1962.
5 Hauswirtschaftliche Berufsschulen.
6 Landwirtschaftliche Berufsschulen.
7 Gewerbliche Berufsschulen.
8 Kaufmännische Berufsschulen.
9 At the time of writing, there are 311 recognized skilled trades in industry, and 120 semi-skilled trades in the Federal Republic.
10 About 70 per cent of all young workers in Germany are classifiable as apprentices or trainees.
11 It was announced in August 1965 that courses were to be set up for the Royal Society of Health's new examination in Parentcraft and Home-manage-

ment. The first institutions to offer courses for this examination will be the Cheetham Further Education Centre, Manchester; Caernarvonshire Technical College; Basingstoke Technical College; and the South Wiltshire College of Further Education.

12 'Prospects for the Newsom Boy', paper delivered to the British Association on 1 September, 1964 by D. M. Downes; see also D. M. Downes and F. Flower, *Educating for Uncertainty*, the Fabian Society, 1965.

CHAPTER 8

1 This survey of technical schools (and the survey of vocational schools in the preceding chapter) is based, to a large extent, on the author's knowledge or experience of such schools as they exist in the state of Baden-Württemberg. The organization of the system as a whole is similar throughout West Germany, although there are likely to be some different features in the various states.

2 In the Netherlands over one-third of the total elementary school population transfers to the junior technical schools at the age of twelve, where an important place in the curriculum is allotted to pre-occupational training.

One of the features of the Rahmenplan of 14 February 1959 was the proposal that in the ninth elementary school year, which was to be introduced, the pupils should receive the knowledge and skills, including those of a technical nature, which would serve them in their later lives as workers. Since 1960 Hesse, for instance, has organized ninth-year experimental classes of several types. Some of these classes hold one-third of their teaching time in the vocational schools; other experimental classes still give all their teaching in the elementary schools, although vocational school teachers are drafted in to give instruction in practical work in the workshops.

3 Berufsfachschule.
4 Fachschulen.
5 Technikerschulen.
6 Höhere Fachschulen.
7 Ingenieurschulen.
8 Kaufmännische Berufsfachschulen/Handelsschulen.
9 Höhere Handelsschulen.
10 Wirtschaftsoberschule.
11 Haushaltungsschulen.
12 Frauenfachschulen.
13 Landwirtschaftschulen.
14 Höhere Landbauschulen.
15 'Der zweite Bildungsweg'.
16 As early as 1938 the Technical High School (Technische Oberschule) in Stuttgart took in its first students, former elementary or middle school pupils,

who, having left school, had continued their education in the vocational and technical schools. This college prepares its students for the Abitur examination, so that, if they wish, they may proceed to university study. The concept of this type of college, which is an essential feature of the 'zweiter Bildungsweg', has now been generally recognized and institutions of similar standing are now being introduced in other states. The first of these institutions in Hesse, for example (Hessenkollegs), was founded in Wiesbaden in 1959.

17 See Ernst Bornemann and Hans Böttcher, 'Der Jugendliche und seine Freizeit – Chancen und Gefährdungen', *Psychologische Rundschau*, July 1964.

CHAPTER 9

1 Great Britain Board of Education, *Compulsory Continuation Schools in Germany* by H. A. Clay, p. 23, H.M.S.O., 1910.

2 *Trade and Technical Education in France and Germany*, report by J. C. Snail for London County Council, 1914.

3 Quoted, op. cit., p. 9.

4 Op. cit. p. 9.

5 A comprehensive survey of the work achieved by this Institute is given in F. E. Foden's thesis: 'A history of technical examinations in England to 1918, with special reference to the examination work of the City and Guilds of London Institute', Reading, 1960.

6 For more details see the following theses: A. H. Thomas, 'Compulsory day continuation schools between 1919 and 1939, with special reference to London', Newcastle, 1945; K. Brooksbank, 'The day continuation school in England', Manchester, 1939; I. F. Rolls, 'Present trends in part-time day release schemes in further education', London, 1960.

7 *Education Act, 1944*, Section 41.

8 Op. cit., Section 43, subsection 1.

9 Op. cit., Section 44, subsection 3.

10 *Training boys in industry: the non-apprentice*, Section 1, para. 2, Industrial Training Council, 1960.

11 See *Training for Skill: Recruitment and training of young workers in industry* (Carr report), para. 47, H.M.S.O., 1958.

12 The French FPA courses (Formation Professionelle des Adultes) have achieved great success in this field.

13 In England much valuable work is achieved by various organizations such as the W.E.A., evening institutes and university extra-mural departments, although the number of participants at these courses is considerably lower than that regarding the German Volkschochschule.

14 *Das Grundaxiom des Bildungsprozesses und seine Folgerungen für die Schulorganisation*, Berlin (Union).

15 Op. cit., 3rd edn, p. 48.
16 *Theorie der Bildung*, p. 17., Teubner, 1926.
17 *Die Seele des Erziehers und das Problem der Lehrerbildung*, 8th edn, p. 35., Oldenbourg, 1961.
18 *Theorie der Bildung*, p. 213, Teubner, 1926.
19 Op. cit., p. 218.
20 *Die Seele des Erziehers und das Problem der Lehrerbildung*, Teubner.
21 *Autorität und Freiheit als Bildungsgrundsätze*, Oldenbourg.
22 *Theorie der Bildung*, Teubner.
23 *Theorie der Bildungsorganisation*, Teubner, 1933.
24 In March 1966, after this book had been written, it was announced that the professional training, received in Russia during the period of secondary education, was to be continued only in those schools which possessed proper and adequate facilities for this training.
25 *Day Release: the report of a committee set up by the Minister of Education*, H.M.S.O., 1964.
26 Foreword to *Day Release for Clerical Workers*, National Federation of Professional Workers, 1965.
27 Op. cit., para. 58, sect. *b*.
28 *Industrial Training Act*, 1964, Section 2.

Index

aims of education, 14, 25–9, 30–2, 34–5, 50–2, 131
apprentice examinations, 104, 108, 136
Aristotle, 35, 43
attendance laws, 17, 18, 19, 20, 22, 23, 27, 37, 71, 74–5, 76, 79, 83, 84, 86, 92, 99, 102, 122, 124, 136
Augsburg, 4, 5, 7
Austrian trade schools, 69–70

Baden, 20, 22, 37, 73
Bavaria, 15, 23, 24, 26, 70, 82
Bismarck, 22

Central Office for Vocational Training, 127
'classes pilotes', 63
Comenius, Johann Amos, 17, 18
Crowther Report, 137
curriculi (of Kerschensteiner's continuation schools), 52–5, 56–9, 61, 75, 76–7, 81, 84–5, 105
curriculi (of other schools), 17, 18, 22, 37, 38, 78, 80, 83, 95, 96–7, 101, 102, 112, 116, 117

day-release in England, 136–8
Dewey, John, 82
Dickson, Alec, 67

Education Act, 1918, 122
Education Act, 1944, 123–4
elementary school, 2, 14–16, 17, 19, 22, 24, 26, 31–2, 35, 36, 48, 49, 50, 60, 64, 66, 71, 74, 75, 77, 80, 83, 101, 106, 108, 112, 119, 121
Erlangen, 9

extension courses, 110, 119
extra-curricular activities, 65, 76, 82

Fachschulreife, 119
Fichte, Johann Gottlieb, 29
Francke, August Hermann, 18
Folk High Schools, 128

Goethe, Johann Wolfgang von, 43, 70
Gordan, Paul, 9
Government Training Centres, 127
Gymnasium, 5–6, 8–9, 10, 48–9, 62, 64, 101, 111, 112, 113, 115, 119

Heimatkunde, 37
Herbart, Johann Friedrich, 26, 38
Hesse, 22
history, value of, 56–8
home influence, 84, 101
Humboldt, Karl Wilhelm von, 20–1

Industrial Training Act, 138

Kerschensteiner, Anton, 1, 7
Kerschensteiner, Georg, *Works:*
  Authority and Freedom as Educational Principles, 133
  Basic Questions of School Organisation, 31, 39, 50, 52, 53, 57, 64, 68, 83
  Character and Value of the Sciences, 80
  Character and Character Training, 45, 46, 47, 83
  Concept of Education for Citizenship, 83
  Concept of the Activity School, 30, 31–2, 83
  Considerations on the Curriculum, 15, 25–7, 36
  Development of Artistic Talent, 78
  Fundamentals of the Educational Process and their Consequences for School Organisation, 130
  Observations and Comparisons concerning Technical Education outside Bavaria, 69
  Organisation and Curriculi of the Compulsory Continuation and Technical Schools for Boys in Munich, 55, 83
  Prize Essay: German Youth and Education for Citizenship, 24, 25, 28, 31, 33–5, 38, 42, 48, 56, 57, 59, 61–2, 68, 83, 128, 129

Kerschensteiner, Georg, *Works (contd.)*:
   Soul of the Educator and the Problem of Teacher Training, 132
   Theory of Education, 40, 133
   Theory of Educational Organisation, 133
Kerschensteiner, Josef, 3
Kerschensteiner, Katherina, 1, 7
Kerschensteiner, Sophie, 7, 10, 129

laboratories, 61, 76, 80
Lange, Friedrich, 29
Leipzig, 37, 73
Luther, Martin, 16–17
Lycée technique, 134

middle school, 112, 115

nationalism, 29–30, 38, 91–2
Nietzsche, Friedrich, 29
number of schools, 74, 88, 120
number of hours instruction, 74, 94, 96, 106, 107, 113
Nürnberg, 8–10, 39

observation, 46, 78, 80

Realschulen, 18
Rücklin, Friedrich, 37, 38
Russian reforms, 134

Saxony, 22
Schleiermacher, Ludwig, 12
Schweinfurt, 10–12, 39, 72, 79
social service, 66–8
Swedish schools, 134
Swiss apprentice workshops, 70

teacher training, 3, 5, 8, 9, 93, 96, 116, 121
technical and vocational schools (incl. all part-time further education):
   agricultural vocational schools, 93, 102
   continuation schools (Kerschensteiner's), 36, 37, 42, 50–61, 64–6, 72–3, 74–7, 81, 84–6, 105–6, 120–1, 128
   commercial schools, 112–13

technical and vocational schools (*contd.*):
  commercial vocational schools, 93, 97–100, 101
  county colleges, 124
  day continuation schools, 122–3
  domestic vocational schools, 93, 100–2
  economics high school, 113
  engineering schools, 111
  general continuation schools, 21–5, 36, 37, 39–42, 50, 51, 69, 75
  general continuation schools (Kerschensteiner's), 75
  higher technical schools, 110–11, 112–13, 116
  industrial and trades vocational schools, 93–7, 98, 99
  pre-occupational schools, 106–7, 112, 114, 115
  regional vocational schools, 94
  schools for housekeeping, 114
  specialized vocational schools, 94, 98
  Sunday schools, 17, 19, 20, 21, 22, 23
  technical high school/Kolleg, 145–6
  technical schools (in the past), 18, 20
  technical schools (modern), 108–10, 112, 114, 116–19
  technical schools for agriculture, 116
  technical schools for women's professions, 114
  technical schools, 110
  technical universities, 18, 106, 111
  trade schools, 19–20, 69, 77
trade classifications, 127
training of the will, 45, 48, 51

universities, 21, 63, 129
unskilled workers, 75, 99–100, 132

Wandervögel, 29
Weimar, 17, 78
workers' hostels, 128–9
Württemberg, 17, 19, 23
Würzburg, 10

For Product Safety Concerns and Information please contact our EU
representative GPSR@taylorandfrancis.com
Taylor & Francis Verlag GmbH, Kaufingerstraße 24, 80331 München, Germany

www.ingramcontent.com/pod-product-compliance
Lightning Source LLC
Chambersburg PA
CBHW070620300426
44113CB00010B/1594